WONDERS OF THE WORLD

ANDES MOUNTAINS

Rose Blue and Corinne Naden

Technical Consultant

Dr. Robert E. Ford
College of Natural Resources
Utah State University

RAINTREE
STECK-VAUGHN
PUBLISHERS
The Steck-Vaughn Company

Austin, Texas

The authors thank Claire White of Westport, Connecticut, for her helpful descriptions of southernmost South America on her early 1993 trip to Antarctica and vicinity.

Copyright © 1995 by Raintree Steck-Vaughn Publishers.
All rights reserved. No part of the material protected by this copyright may be reproduced or utilized in any form or by any means, electronic or mechanical, including photocopying, recording, or by any information storage and retrieval system, without permission in writing from the copyright owner. Requests for permission to make copies of any part of the work should be mailed to: Copyright Permission, Raintree Steck-Vaughn Publishers, P.O. Box 26015, Austin, TX 78755

A production of B&B Publishing, Inc.

Editor – Jean B. Black
Photo Editor – Margie Benson
Computer Specialist – Katy O'Shea
Interior Design – Scott Davis

Raintree Steck-Vaughn Publishing Staff

Project Editor – Helene Resky
Project Manager – Joyce Spicer

LIBRARY OF CONGRESS CATALOGING-IN-PUBLICATION DATA

Blue, Rose, and Corinne Naden
    Andes mountains / Rose Blue and Corinne Naden
      p. cm. — (Wonders of the world)
    Includes bibliographical references and index.
    ISBN 0-8114-6363-X
    1. Andes — Juvenile literature. 2. Natural history — Andes Region —
Juvenile literature. 3. Environmental protection — Andes Region —
Juvenile literature. [1. Andes.] I. Naden, Corinne J. II. Title. III. Series.
F2212.B58 1995   94-3028
980 — dc20   CIP
                                                                                          AC

Cover photo	Title page photo	Table of Contents page photo
The Urubamba Valley of Peru	The Andes Mountains in Colombia	The Andes Mountains rise behind Ushuaia, Argentina, the southernmost city in the world.

PHOTO SOURCES

Cover Photo: © Brian Vikander

© Walt Anderson: 49
Embassy of Chile: 7, 9 top right, 12 top, 13, 43 both, 45 bottom, 50, 55 bottom
Dr. Clark Erickson: 19 top, 34 top, 56 top
Food and Agriculture Organization photo by
    Peyton Johnson: 48 bottom
Food and Agriculture Organization photo by
    C. Flint: 52 top
Food and Agriculture Organization photo by
    J. Van Acker: 28 left
Food and Agriculture Organization photo by
    H. Null: 45 top
Food and Agriculture Organization photo by
    F. de Borhegyi: 51 top
Dr. Robert Ford: 10, 11, 12 left, 16 top, 17, 35, 36, 37 both, 38 both, 39, 41
Carrol Henderson: 9 left, 19 bottom, 21 both, 22 top, 23, 25 top, 28 top, 30, 31, 32, 53 bottom, 55 top, 60 both
Gary Kramer: 15 top, 47 both, 57, 61
Library of Congress: 24 top

Charles Munn: 34 bottom
© Robert Perron: 26
Embassy of Peru: 16 right both
Probe International/Peggy Hallaward: 52 bottom
© Kevin Schafer: 56 bottom
© Eugene Schulz: 5
Fred Siskind: 58 bottom
© Joy Spurr: 44
© Sylvia Stevens: 3, 9 bottom, 18, 29
Judy Turner: 1, 15 bottom
Lisa Turner: 4, 14, 25 bottom
UN Photo 139457: 40
UN Photo 143385: 20
UN Photo 148007/Jean Pierre Laffont: 59
UN Photo 153323: 58 top
UN Photo 153873/Shawn McCutcheon: 22 bottom
United States Drug Enforcement Agency: 51 bottom
Courtesy West Point Museum Collections, United States
    Military Academy: 24 bottom
Dr. Mike Wolfe: 6, 48 top, 53 top, 54

Printed and bound in the United States of America.
1 2 3 4 5 6 7 8 9 10 VH 99 98 97 96 95 94

Table of Contents

Chapter One
Cordillera of the Andes
4

Chapter Two
The Making of South America
14

Chapter Three
Northern Andes
Venezuela • Colombia • Ecuador
25

Chapter Four
Central Andes
Peru • Bolivia
33

Chapter Five
Southern Andes
Chile • Argentina
42

Chapter Six
Are the Andes in Danger?
50

Glossary
62

For More Information
62

Index
63

Chapter One

Cordillera of the Andes

They are very long, very high, and, as mountains go, very young. They are the Cordillera de los Andes, or Andes Mountains, of South America. In Spanish, *cordillera* means "great mountain chain."

The narrow, curving shape of the Andes is more than 4,500 miles (7,241 km) long, making it the longest mountain system on Earth. However, it is generally not more than 500 miles (805 km) wide.

This chain of mountains forms the western border of South America. The Andes Mountains start in the cold, restless waters of the Antarctic Ocean at Tierra del Fuego, which is an archipelago, or chain of islands, off the southern tip of South America. The islands belong half to Chile and half to Argentina. Ferdinand Magellan is credited with their discovery in 1520. Because he saw smoke when he landed—probably natives sending signals about his arrival—he gave the area its name, which in Spanish means "land of fire." In this wild and remote region, the Andes chain rises from the churning sea and takes a sharp turn.

The mountains continue into Argentina and Bolivia, hugging the Pacific shores of Chile and Peru, and turn to the northeast through Ecuador. From there, the Andes broaden out into Colombia

"When we reached the crest and looked backwards, a glorious view was presented. The atmosphere resplendently clear; the sky an intense blue; the profound valleys; the wild broken forms; the heaps of ruins, piled up during the lapse of ages; the bright-colored rocks, contrasted with the quiet mountains of snow; all these together produced a scene no one could have imagined."

— Charles Darwin in the Andes Mountains

Cape Horn is the southern tip of the Andes *(right)*. The rough seas and almost perpetual storms of the area made "rounding the Horn" difficult for sailing ships.

A ferry takes cars and passengers across the Strait of Magellan from Punta Arenas, Chile, to Tierra del Fuego.

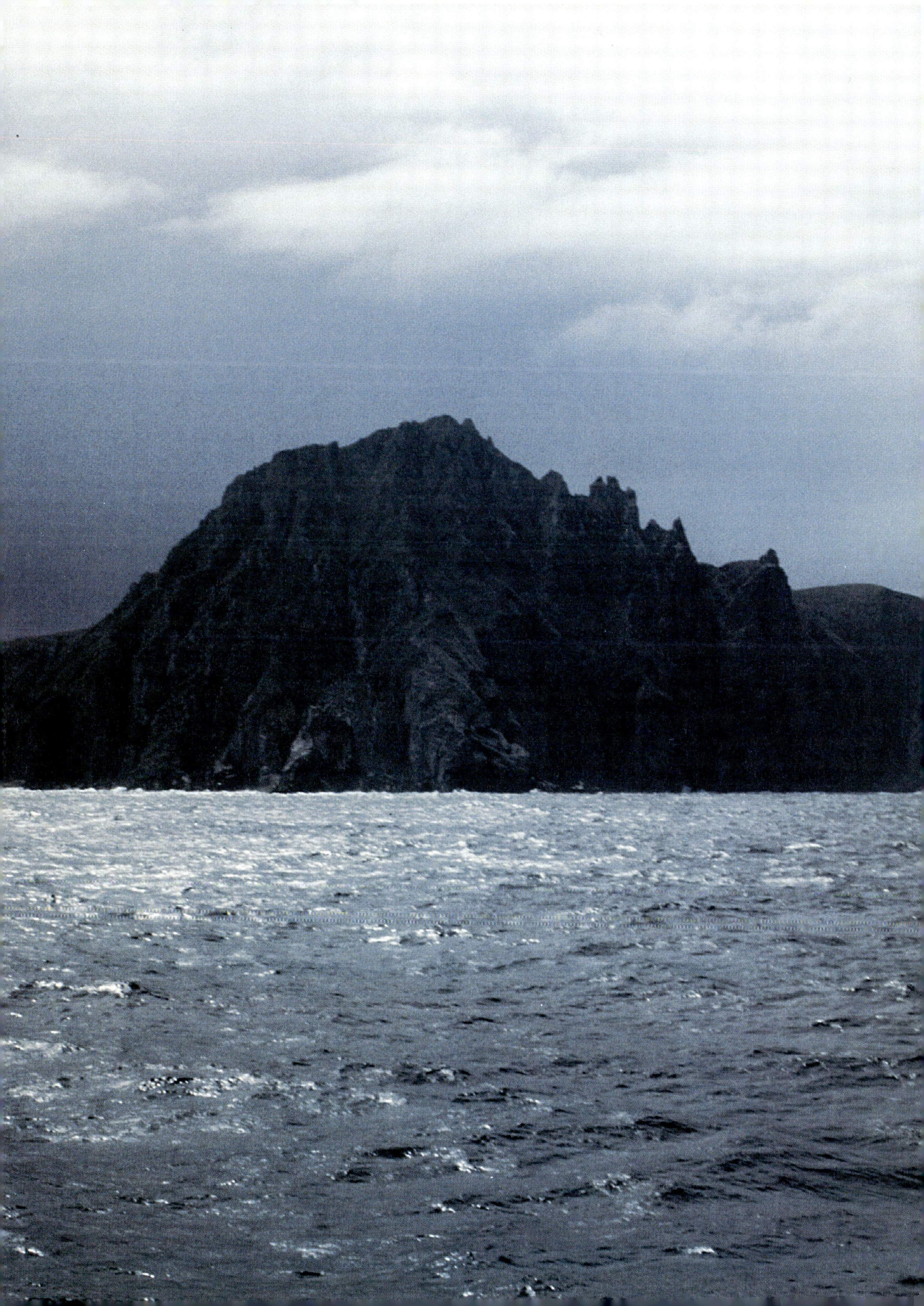

and Venezuela and are brought to a halt by the sunny coast of the Caribbean Sea in the north.

The Andes boast the highest mountain peak in the Western Hemisphere. Snowcapped Aconcagua in Argentina, about 65 miles (105 km) north of Santiago, Chile, soars to a height of 22,831 feet (6,961 m). It was first climbed in 1897. Only the Himalayas in south-central Asia have taller mountains than the Andes. Mount Everest, in the Himalayas on the Nepal-Tibet border, is 29,028 feet (8,850 m) high. The Andes, however, have many peaks higher than 22,000 feet (6,707 m) and more peaks over 10,000 feet (3,049 m) high than any other mountain range.

The high ridges of the Andes lure mountain climbers like a magnet. But it is a very dangerous attraction. Charles S. Houston, author of *Going Higher*, agrees. "Above that level [18,000 feet or 5,488 m]," he says, "even fit climbers risk brain damage and possible death when they go up too fast to adapt."

The high ridges of the Andes in Chile lure mountain climbers to experience the breathtaking view.

The Changing Mountains

The many high peaks in the Andes tell something about the age of this mountain system. It may seem strange to talk about the "age" of mountains. They look so solid, so unchanging. Surely they have always been there. But in the way geologists tell time, the Andes Mountains are young. They were thrust up from a deep ocean trough about 60 to 75 million years ago. That is very young compared, for instance, to the Appalachian Mountains in the eastern United States. The age of the Appalachian Mountains is counted in hundreds of millions of years. So the Andes are a long way from old age. They are still growing and changing. The Rocky Mountains in western North America are about the same age as the Andes.

Earthquakes and volcanic eruptions often occur in the Andes. Many high peaks in this chain are active volcanoes. With its snow-topped cone, Sangay in central Ecuador is the most active volcano in the Andes. It has been spewing out lava, steam, and ash for centuries. Although it is listed at 17,159 feet (5,231 m), the volcano is still growing because of all the eruptions.

Osorno volcano in central Chile is an extinct volcano. It and three other extinct volcanoes form a semi-circle of snow-covered volcanic cones in this region of Chile.

Oddly, the volcanoes of the Andes occur in two separate regions, separated by about 1,000 miles (1,609 km) of gentler land. Sangay is located on the southern edge of the northern group of volcanoes. Aconcagua is located in the northern area of the southern group of volcanoes. These peaks form part of the so-called Ring of Fire, a great circle formed by volcanoes that rim the Pacific Ocean.

In young mountain systems like the Andes, earthquakes and volcanic eruptions help to build up and change the mountains. In old systems like the Appalachians, erosion—gradual wearing away by wind, water, or glacial ice—is the changing force. Through the centuries, erosion smooths craggy mountain peaks into rounded hills. Sometime in the far distant future, erosion may also grind the rugged Andes down into gentle mountains.

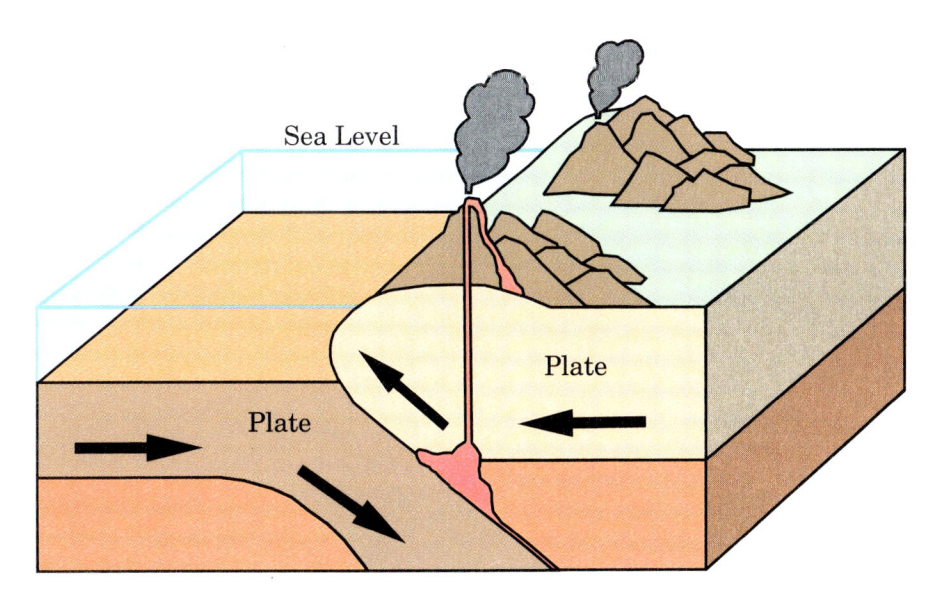

Mountains build when two sections, or plates, of the Earth's crust push against each other, forcing the rock upward. When magma, the molten rock inside the Earth, can escape, it forms volcanoes. The Andes has many active volcanoes.

SOUTH AMERICA AND THE ANDES
National Capital
City (type size indicates city size)
Mountain Peak
0 250 500 miles
0 250 500 kilometers
Caribbean Sea
Cristobal Colón
18,947 ft (5,777m)
SIERRA DE PERIJÁ
L. Maracaibo
CORDILLERA DE MÉRIDA
Pico Bolívar
16,411 ft (5,003m)
Caracas
ISTHMUS OF PANAMA
Gulf of Panama
CORDILLERA OCCIDENTAL
CORDILLERA CENTRAL
CORDILLERA ORIENTAL
Bogotá
LLANOS
VENEZUELA
GUYANA
Georgetown
Paramaribo
SURINAME
FR. GUIANA (Fr.)
Cayenne
Atlantic Ocean
COLOMBIA
ECUADOR
Quito
Cotopaxi
19,347 ft (5,898m)
SIERRA
Iquitos
PERU
Amazon R.
Amazon R.
BRAZIL
CORDILLERA OCCIDENTAL
CORDILLERA CENTRAL
CORDILLERA ORIENTAL
Huascarán
22,205 ft (6,770m)
Lima
BOLIVIA
CORD. REAL
L. Titicaca
Illimani
20,741 ft (6,322m)
La Paz
Arequipa
Sajama
21,463 ft (6,542m)
Sucre
Brasilia
PARAGUAY
Asunción
Antofagasta
CORDILLERA DE LOS ANDES
Ojos del Salado
22,572 ft (6,882m)
Pacific Ocean
ARGENTINA
CHILE
PAMPAS
URUGUAY
Aconcagua
22,831 ft (6959m)
Santiago
Montevideo
Buenos Aires
Rio de la Plata
Concepción
Atlantic Ocean
PATAGONIA
ANDES DE PATAGONIA
Gulf of San Matias
Gulf of San Jorge
TIERRA DEL FUEGO
Antarctic Ocean
Strait of Magellan
CAPE HORN
Antarctic Ocean

Land of Extremes

On a map, the Andes look like a long, continuous chain. Actually, this massive mountain system is a series of loosely connected ranges with depressions and lofty plateaus in between. The Andes chain contains many extremes, from majestic glaciers to flat, broad plateaus, from sunny grasslands to cloud-covered peaks, from deserts to high mountain lakes. The highest navigable lake in the world, Lake Titicaca on the Peru-Bolivia border, is located in the Andes at an elevation of 12,507 feet (3,813 m). The portion in Peru alone covers 1,914 square miles (4,957 sq km) and is the largest lake in Peru.

The climate of the Andes is greatly influenced by the Humboldt Current, also called the Peru Current, which flows northward from the Antarctic along the western coast of South America. The chill that it brings to the atmosphere makes the coasts of the countries bordering the Pacific Ocean very dry.

Under normal conditions the Equatorial Counter

Native to South America, the llama has long been used as a pack animal to carry passengers and cargo over rugged mountain trails. Llamas can cover 15 to 20 miles (24 to 32 km) per day under a full load.

The Valley of the Moon in Chile showcases beautiful desert formations.

Parts of the Andes have permanent glaciers. The ice is perpetually moving, grinding down the rock of the mountains. This is a glacier in the Chilean Andes.

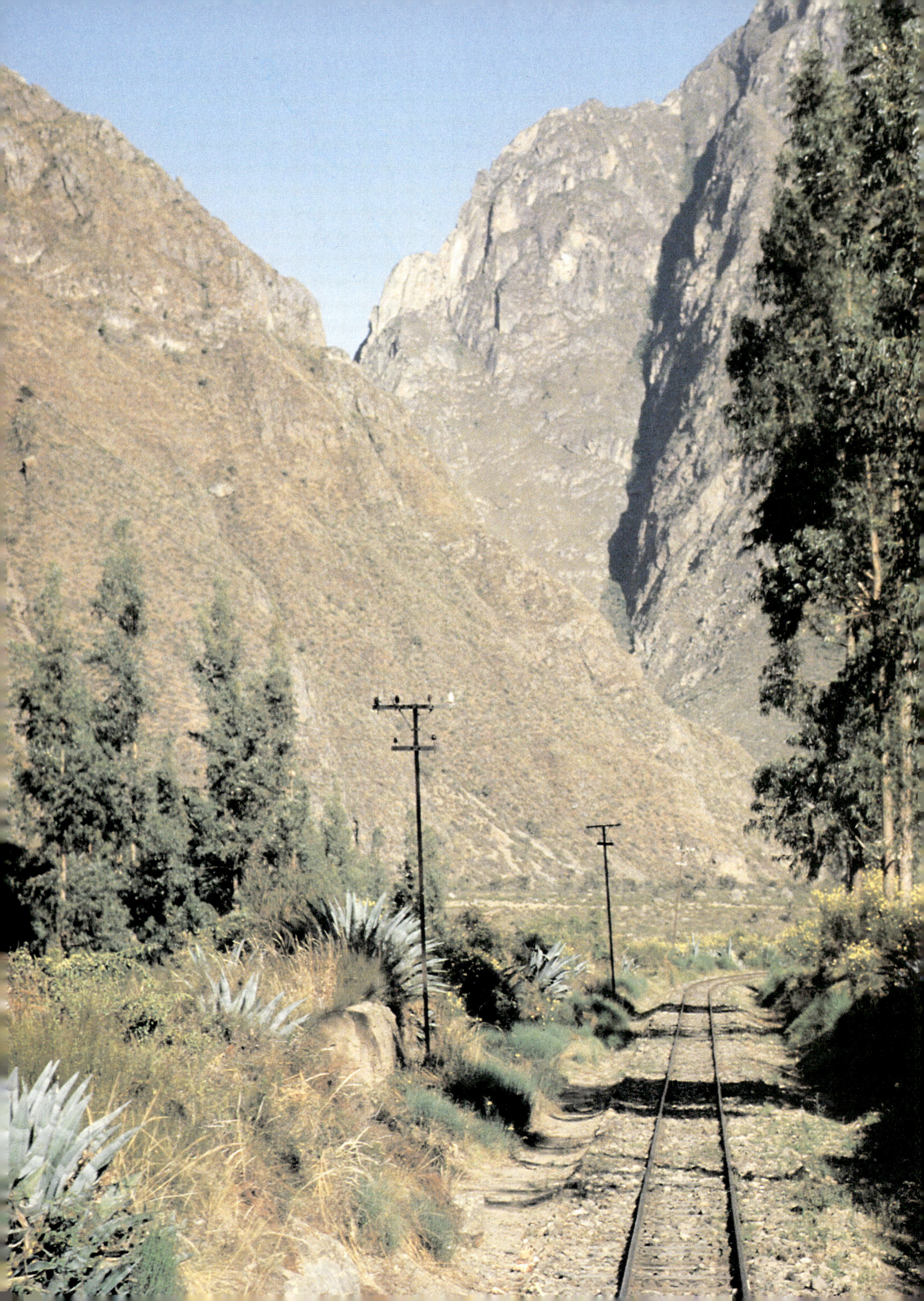

Narrow-gauge railroads provide the only modern transportation to the highest regions of the Andes. This railroad line *(left)* runs through the Urubamba Canyon in Peru from Cuzco to Machu Picchu.

Current—flowing from west to east—is rather weak. Under unusual circumstances, this current gets stronger and much warmer, due to climactic and oceanic phenomena scientists don't understand yet. This warm water flows toward South America where it penetrates the much colder Humboldt Current. When this occurs, the dramatic change in ocean temperature affects aquatic systems, sometimes producing "red tides" and disturbing normal rainfall patterns. This unusual warming begins near Christmas, so it is called El Niño, Spanish for "the Christ Child." It only happens, however, about once in every five years on an irregular basis.

Parts of the Andes that are normally desert may have heavy rainfall during El Niño, while other regions that normally have sufficient rainfall experience drought. Usually, the waters off South America provide abundant fishing, especially tuna and anchovies, because the Humboldt Current brings nutrients from deep in the ocean up to the surface. However, fishing decreases substantially during El Niño, because the increased temperature reduces the normal nutrients and oxygen levels. This kills much of the microscopic animal and plant life that tuna and other organisms feed on.

This highway to the ancient Inca ruins of Machu Picchu in Peru has to wind long distances back and forth in order to climb the steep vertical mountains.

High in the Andes, winter can be deadly because of its unusual cold and snow. Many scientists think that the ancient Inca and Moche civilizations of the Andes disappeared partly because of catastrophes related to climate changes caused by El Niño.

The Andes Mountains separate the narrow western coastal plain from the rest of South America. Throughout the centuries, transportation and communication have been difficult in these highlands. In early years, the forbidding Andes kept away would-be invading tribes from the eastern part of the continent.

The city of Iquitos is just over 600 miles (966 km) northeast of Lima, almost the same distance as between New York City and Detroit, Michigan. New Yorkers can drive to Detroit in a day—but they don't have to cross the Andes. To avoid the 600-mile (966-km) mountain route in the days before the airplane, travelers in Peru very often left Iquitos, went east down the Amazon River to the Atlantic Ocean, north to the Caribbean Sea, through the Isthmus of Panama, and south down the Pacific Coast to Lima—a distance of 7,000 miles (11,263 km)!

Roads and railroads are expensive to build and difficult to maintain. The Central Railway, on the western slopes of Peru and Bolivia, is the highest standard-gauge railroad in the world. It operates at more than 15,800 feet (4,817 m) above sea level.

If the land of the Andes offers many extremes, so does its weather. When the sun sets in the highlands, the summer warmth of midday turns to bone-chilling winter. There is almost no rainfall in some parts of the Andes—and frequent tropical downpours in others. In terms of land and climate, the Andes Mountains have something for everyone.

El Tatio Geyser Field in Chile is one of the world's most active geyser regions. Located high in the Andes, the region is surrounded by active volcanoes.

The Inca people built two great roads, each over 2,000 miles (3,218 km) in length. One highway ran near the coastal regions, and the other was built in the Andes. The photo below shows a portion of the inland Inca Trail with a footbridge along the Urubama River in Peru.

Spectacular Torres del Paine National Park (right) is known for its scenic peaks, glaciers, lakes, and wildlife. There are 105 species of birds in the park, including the Andean condor.

12

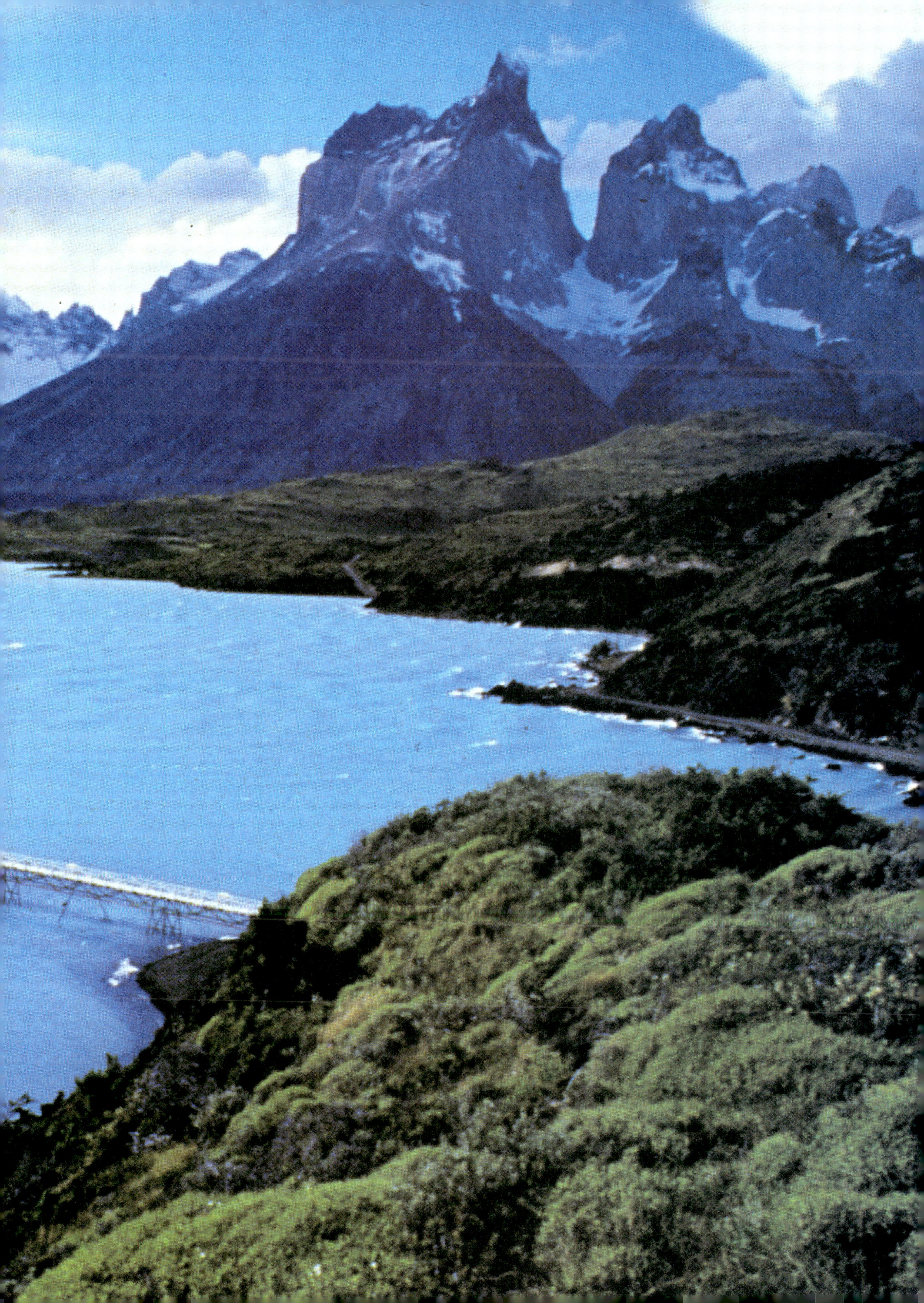

Chapter Two

The Making of South America

South America looks like a lopsided triangle. With an area of nearly 7 million square miles (18,830,000 sq km), it is the fourth largest of the world's continents—smaller than Asia, Africa, and North America and larger than Antarctica, Europe, and Australia.

South America is so long that the equator runs through its northern part and ice-bound Antarctica lies close to its southern tip. In the east, great plateaus are divided by the Amazon River Basin, the largest in the world. Second in length only to Africa's Nile, the mighty Amazon River begins as mountain streams high in the Andes and flows nearly 4,000 miles (6,440 km) across Brazil to its mouth at the Atlantic Ocean.

In the southeast is the Pampas, or Pampa, of Argentina. This enormous level plain—almost 300,000 square miles (776,940 sq km)—gets its name from an Amerindian word meaning "flat surface." It is a monotonous landscape formed over the centuries from rocks and soil tumbling down the slopes of the Andes. Once a barren wilderness, the Pampas has now been fully developed for agriculture.

South of the Pampas is the largest dry spot in

Other than the Andes, the major feature of South America is the vast Amazon River Basin. But the two are connected because the source of the river is in the mountains. This photo shows the upper reaches of the Amazon in eastern Ecuador.

The town of Esquel, Argentina, is located in Patagonia, a region where few people live.

the Americas—the Patagonian Desert. This large area covers most of southern Argentina. The name *Patagonia* is derived from the Spanish word that means "big feet." The Amerindians who lived here before Europeans arrived were quite tall and wore big bootlike shoes full of grass.

The rest of South America is entirely dominated by the long curving line of the Andes. The look of the continent today is the result of powerful forces that thrust up this enormous mountain chain millions of years ago.

It is hard to describe the Andes as a whole because the chain is so long and so different from region to region. The mountains are an important part of seven nations—Venezuela, Colombia, Ecuador, Peru, Bolivia, Chile, and Argentina. The Andes chain in Venezuela, Colombia, and Ecuador is made up of several side-by-side ranges that branch out to the Caribbean. These mountains are generally low to moderately high.

The central Andes of Peru and Bolivia are much wider than the mountains in Ecuador. The chain is widest in Bolivia. Instead of side-by-side mountains, the central Andes form a huge, high mass of rugged peaks and broad valleys. Lake Titicaca is located here, as are many active volcanoes.

From Bolivia, along the Chile-Argentina border, the southern Andes begin to narrow, becoming a single range with some of the loftiest peaks in the entire system. This is also a region of active volcanoes. Farther south, near the southern tip of the continent, the Andes are much lower, decreasing in height until they seem to tumble into the sea.

In Colombia and Venezuela, the Andes Mountains are not as high as in Peru or Bolivia. Small farms, such as the one shown below in Colombia, are located in the mountains and valleys.

Even today, when only the remains of the Inca city of Machu Picchu are visible, it's clear that this Andean city (in what is now Peru) was a magnificent focus of the empire. Discovered in 1911, it is thought that this city was a royal retreat for the Inca emperor Pachacuti.

An Inca pottery vase

The handle of this gold ceremonial knife represents a male idol.

The Inca Empire

About 20,000 years ago, nomads entered North America, probably from Siberia into Alaska. They eventually reached South America through the Isthmus of Panama. Human bones have been found in the Andes that are about 12,000 years old, but scientists believe people arrived there much earlier than that.

Through the centuries, the forbidding barrier of the Andes kept away many outsiders. Local cultures developed and died out. Little is known of them. These early peoples, unlike the Aztecs and Maya in Central America and Mexico, did not develop a system of writing or a calendar. They were mainly hunters and fishers, and they left no written records. Their history is known only from the ancient buildings that have been uncovered by archaeologists, local traditions, and tales written or told by the first European explorers.

CHILDREN TO PLEASE THE GODS

The main god of the Incas was Viracocha, creator of the Earth, people, and animals. Worship focused on elaborate temples and shrines. The most famous is the Sun Temple, which still stands in Cuzco. The temples housed the Inca priests, who were honored and feared. They held great power over everyone, and the high priest at Cuzco had more power than anyone. Important Inca rituals included sacrifice, both of animals and humans. On every special occasion, animals were slaughtered at the shrines to appease the gods and bring good fortune to the people. But in times of great need—drought and famine, or after defeat in battle—more extreme measures were called for. As many as 200 children at a time might be thrown into temple fires to please the gods and chase away ill fortune. In the historic Bolivian town of Tihuanaco, ruins of an old Inca temple, where human sacrifice took place, show sculpted faces in the wall *(right)*.

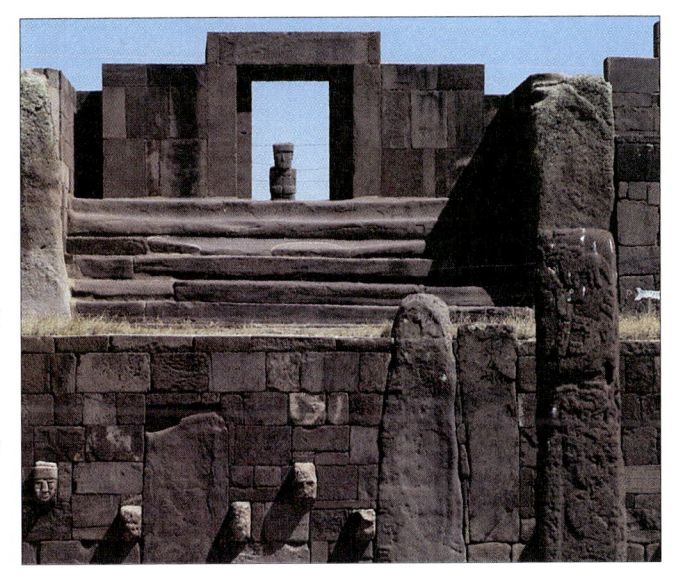

Amazing tales they were! To the surprise of travelers from Spain, who reached what is now Peru in 1532, they found an advanced, thriving civilization. This was the Inca Empire, perhaps the most remarkable of all the early peoples of South America. With a genius for political organization, the Inca united all the people in an area that extended south to Chile and Argentina and north to Colombia—or about the same distance as from New York City to the Panama Canal. Starting in the 1400s, the Incas controlled about 12 million people who spoke 20 or more different languages. The capital city, Cuzco, high in the Andes of central Peru, was called the "City of the Sun." Today, Cuzco has a population of about 275,000.

The highly organized and stable Inca Empire lasted for several centuries. But within 40 years after Columbus landed in the Americas, the empire crumbled. It ended in 1532, brought down by fewer than 200 Spaniards with guns.

The People Today

Like their great mountain system, the people of South America differ from land to land and region to region. They are a mixture of nationalities, races, and native peoples. Spanish and Portuguese are the principal languages, but millions of South Americans speak the Amerindian languages of Quechua and Aymara. For them, Spanish is a foreign tongue.

The people of modern South America may be divided into several groups. Amerindians are descendants of the societies that were living in South America when the Europeans invaded. Iberians can trace their ancestors to the early Spanish and Portuguese colonizers. The ancestors of modern-day Africans in South America were the first slaves brought in by the Europeans in the 1500s. Immigrants came from Europe mainly during the late nineteenth century, continuing until about 1930. Mestizos are people of mixed heritage.

Living high in the Andes north of Quito, Ecuador, the Otavalo people claim to be the only pure Ecuadorian Amerindians. Known for the beautiful woven fabrics they sell in the market at Otavalo, they are a prosperous group who wear distinctive clothing.

About one-third of the entire population of South America lives in the Andes. Many people from the mountains and other rural areas seek a better life in the mushrooming cities. What most of them find, however, are all the problems that overcrowding brings.

Even though life is hard in the high wilderness, more than 20 million Andes dwellers are true mountain people. They keep to their old ways and customs, ignoring the fact that the twenty-first century is almost upon us. It is easy to do. The world of those who live in the high Andes is small and enclosed. Few outsiders just "drop by."

Most people begin to feel some effects of the lack of oxygen at only 10,000 feet (3,050 m). Veteran mountain climber, photographer, and Andes expert Loren McIntyre says, "It has taken me days or weeks to adjust every time I tackle Andean mountains higher than 18,000 feet (5,500 m). At that elevation, air pressure is half what it is at sea level and a normal breath brings only half the normal amount of oxygen to the lungs."

But numerous Andean natives live at altitudes up to 17,000 feet (5,200 m). Their bodies have developed some adaptations that keep them safe. Their lungs are bigger than most people's, so more oxygen goes in on each breath, and the heart is 20 percent larger. In addition, their red blood cells are bigger than most people's, so each cell carries more oxygen. Oddly enough, an Andean native who goes to live on the plains soon loses these adaptations.

The modern-day inhabitants of the Andes are descendants of the Incas and other early peoples in South America. The largest group is known as the Quechua, after the language they speak.

The name of the Andes Mountains may have come from *anta*, a Quechua word that means "copper." The Andes are rich in copper ore, as well as in silver, tin, gold, and other metals. In order to reach this wealth of minerals, many roads and railroads were built in this forbidding land.

The highest mine in the Andes, perhaps in the world, is a sulfur-rich volcano called Aucanquilcha, in northern Chile. The miners work in very thin air

These Quechua people of Bolivia are cooking potatoes in a field oven at 12,500 feet (3,810 m). Their bodies have adapted to life at very high altitudes.

Mestizos—people of mixed blood—make up the majority of the population of South America. This family lives outside Quito, Ecuador.

nearly 4 miles (6.4 km) high. When the snow is deep, they must climb the slopes on foot to reach the mine. At the end of the day, they toboggan down the mountain, heading for home at breakneck speeds.

Most Quechua-speaking Amerindians today live in Peru and Bolivia. They have long been isolated and neglected, though some steps have been taken by both countries since the 1970s to improve their lot. Farming and raising livestock are still their main occupations. By providing more land and instructing them in the use of modern farm tools, the governments of Peru and Bolivia are hoping to bring the Quechua into the mainstream of life.

Amerindians are descendants of the people who lived in South America when Europeans arrived. This Quechua-speaking mother and child live in Peru.

Araucanians are descendants of an early native people who once ruled part of Chile. When the Spanish arrived in the 1500s, they began to push the natives deeper into the forests and away from the fertile lands along the rivers and coasts.

One tribe of Araucanians, called Mapuche, consisted of very strong warriors who resisted the Spanish invasion and sometimes fought against the conquerors. Eventually, however, even the determined Mapuche were forced to give in to the wave of European settlers. Many of the Mapuche adopted the newcomers' farming techniques and have more or less blended into Chilean society.

Farming the Land

In the mountainous terrain of the Andes, specific vegetation grows at specific altitudes, called life zones. From sea level to 2,000 feet (600 m), farmers plant cacao, tobacco, bananas, sugarcane, and corn. Up to 5,000 feet (1,500 m), they also grow coffee. Palm trees and evergreens flourish at this level as well. Between 5,000 and 10,000 feet (1,500 m and 3,000 m), bamboo and tree ferns, wheat, potatoes, and barley grow. Starting at 10,000 feet (3,000 m), above the tree line, the plant life consists mainly of grass and moss and the low vegetation known as lichens, although some potatoes will grow. Above 15,000 feet (4,500 m) is a land of perpetual snow.

On the eastern slopes of the Andes, between about 5,000 feet and 10,000 feet (1,500 m and 3,000 m) is a region called the cloud forest. It is a magical, misty region of perpetual rain and fog. Also called montane rain forest, this area is created by the clashing of rising warm moist air and cold dry mountain breezes. Because the zone is perpetually wet, many moisture-loving plants, such as orchids and bamboo, and animals, such

Cloud forests have many epiphytes—plants that grow on other plants. Bromeliads *(below)* and orchids are epiphytes that grow in these areas.

Tropical evergreen forests called cloud forests occur in the Andes between 5,000 feet (1,500 m) and 10,000 feet (3,050 m). These areas are bathed in continual rain and fog.

The páramos life zone is a treeless region above 10,500 feet (3,200 m).

as hummingbirds, thrive there. Large fir trees grow in the zone, but instead of having thin needles, they may have leaves that are 0.3 inch (0.8 cm) thick.

The problems of modern-day South American native peoples are similar in all the lands of the Andes. The people in the high Andes have mostly been ignored. Too long neglected by their governments and isolated from mainstream society, they are for the most part poorly educated and poorly fed. Their main occupations are farming and raising livestock, often using the same methods as their ancestors did centuries ago. The high Andean people are subsistence farmers, who work small plots of land and raise corn or potatoes or other vegetables for their own families. These mountain farmlands are too poor and too small to enable the people to grow crops for sale.

There have always been problems with agriculture in the Andes. Very little land is suitable for farming. The slopes are steep, the soil is poor, and the climate is harsh. After the arrival of the Spanish, the fertile land along the coast and in the valleys was given to the colonists and divided into huge estates called haciendas. The newcomers brought sheep and cattle with them. These European animals required a very different kind of land than was available in most of the Andes region where the natives had previously used llamas.

An Andean vegetable, the potato, has become one of the world's staple foods. Originating in Peru, it can grow in many different climates. Some can grow in the thin, unfertile soil above 14,000 feet (4,267 m). These Peruvian farmers are harvesting potatoes near Lake Titicaca.

22

The colonists left only the poorest land in the mountains to the native people. This land was badly irrigated and subject to drought. It would not produce enough food for the natives to feed their families, so many went to work on the huge haciendas of the colonists. They farmed without pay but were given food and shelter and perhaps a small plot of land for their own use. In effect, they were little better than slaves.

In the 1960s and 1970s, Peru and other South American republics tried to change some of the old ways. Huge estates were broken up and the land redistributed. Some estates are now run as cooperatives, meaning that those who work the land share the profits. But even with land reforms, many of the farmers are still desperately poor. A better way of life has yet to reach these dwellers in the high Andes.

Haciendas were huge estates developed by Spanish settlers. Entire forests were cut or burned down to create grazing land for cattle and sheep brought from Europe. On this ranch in Venezuela, 26,000 cattle are raised on 106,000 acres (42,930 ha).

Gaining Independence

Over centuries, South America was explored, invaded, conquered, colonized, and controlled, mainly by Spain and Portugal. The native people were called "Indians" by the invaders because Columbus mistakenly thought he had found a route to India, instead of a "New World." The Europeans often forced these natives into slave labor, giving them no freedom and no future.

Revolts by the "Indians," corruption in colonial governments, overworked mines, and unproductive farming methods brought much unrest to the nations of the Andes. By the early 1800s, revolution was in the air. The people wanted independence from their European conquerors.

To speak of independence in South America is to speak mainly of two men—Simón Bolívar, known as "the Liberator," and José de San Martín. Simón Bolívar (1783-1830) was born into a wealthy family in Venezuela. Educated in Europe, he returned to South America in 1807 and rejoiced in Venezuela's independence from Spain in 1810. But when Spain took back his country a year later, Bolívar left for New Granada, now Colombia, to form an army to regain Venezuela's independence.

In 1819, Bolívar engineered one of the most daring of all military battles. He led approximately 2,500 men over rugged Andean peaks, surprising the Spaniards, who believed the mountains could not be crossed. He defeated the larger Spanish force at Boyacá, north of Bogotá, Colombia, and changed the history of northern South America. Venezuela was liberated in 1821, and Ecuador's independence followed two years later.

Simón Bolívar

Bolívar met Argentina-born José de San Martín (1778-1850) in 1822. Although educated in Spain for a military career, San Martín became a great fighter for South American independence. He achieved the liberation of Peru in 1821. When he met Bolívar, it is believed he wanted the Liberator's aid in freeing other South American lands. If so, Bolívar must have said "no," for after the meeting, San Martín returned to Peru and went into exile. He died in France in 1850.

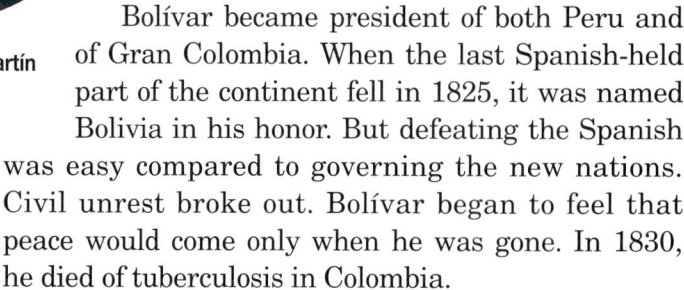

Bolívar became president of both Peru and of Gran Colombia. When the last Spanish-held part of the continent fell in 1825, it was named Bolivia in his honor. But defeating the Spanish was easy compared to governing the new nations. Civil unrest broke out. Bolívar began to feel that peace would come only when he was gone. In 1830, he died of tuberculosis in Colombia.

José de San Martín

The lands that Bolívar and San Martín fought for are still independent Andean nations, each with its own character and life. Let us take a closer look at them separately.

Chapter Three
Northern Andes
Venezuela • Colombia
Ecuador

In northern South America, the Andes Mountains cross Venezuela, Colombia, and Ecuador. From the Caribbean Sea, they branch out across part of Venezuela and western Colombia. Farther south, they cling to the curving western coast of the continent. Although they shrink in width as they enter Ecuador, they cover much of that tiny nation.

Venezuela

Looking at a map, you'll see that the Republic of Venezuela is right on top of the South American continent. Its long northern coastline hugs the Caribbean Sea and Atlantic Ocean. To the east is Guyana, to the south Brazil, to the west Colombia. Twice the size of California, Venezuela covers 352,145 square miles (912,050 sq km). But it has only two-thirds of California's population, or about 20 million people. Venezuela also claims several islands found in the Caribbean Sea.

Venezuela is a land of jungles, mountains, and dry coastal regions. Most of the country consists of forested highlands and lowland plains. Through them—and along the border with Colombia—flows

An old monastery (now converted into a hotel) in the Venezuelan Andes is a reminder of early Spanish colonization.

Mochima National Park is made up of several Venezuelan islands with unusual red sands.

25

the great Orinoco River. But western Venezuela belongs to the Andes.

The Andes mountain system in the north begins at the Caribbean, where the mountains form two branches. The western branch runs along the border with Colombia, it is called the Sierra de Perijá. It is separated from the eastern branch by Lake Maracaibo. In the eastern branch, the Cordillera de Mérida, erosion has uncovered great uplifted blocks of granite, but there are also many snow-covered peaks. Near the center of the range is Venezuela's highest mountain, Pico Bolívar, at 16,411 feet (5,003 m).

Spanish explorers named the country in 1499. In fact, some historians say that it was Amerigo Vespucci who did so. When he saw the houses of the natives built on stilts over water, he called the area "Little Venice," or Venezuela. That was the year after Christopher Columbus, on his third voyage to the "New World," first saw the coastline. The capital, Caracas, was founded in 1567. The oil boom of the 1930s and 1940s brought many people to the city.

LAKE MARACAIBO—LARGE AND SHALLOW

Lake Maracaibo in Venezuela is South America's largest lake—about 5,217 square miles (13,512 sq km). However, around the world at least 17 lakes are larger.

Actually, Lake Maracaibo is a large inlet of the Caribbean Sea with a swampy shoreline. Near its northern end where it meets the sea, the water is salty. Moving south, the water becomes progressively fresher as water pours into the lake from mountain rivers.

As wide as 75 miles (121 km) in some places, Lake Maracaibo is so shallow, except in the south, that ships could not travel on it throughout most of history. Finally, in 1957, a 35-foot (11-km) deep channel was dredged, making the lake accessible to oceangoing vessels. Today, many of those ships are giant oil tankers loading oil for the United States.

The lake has almost disappeared under the thousands of oil derricks on the shore and out 20 miles (32 km) into the lake's waters. Venezuela's largest and richest oil deposits are located under the lake—almost 70 percent of the nation's oil comes from this area.

The country used to export more petroleum than any other country in the world.

Venezuela's petroleum industry was developed and operated by the English, Americans, and Dutch. The government of Venezuela took over its oil industry in 1975.

Only about 2 percent of Venezuela's people are Amerindians. Whites make up about 20 percent, and Africans less than 10 percent. The remainder of the population are *pardo*, a mixture of African, European, and Amerindian ancestry.

In the twentieth century, Venezuela has changed from an agricultural society to one that is much more urban. The change was largely caused by development of the country's huge oil reserves. The oil brought wealth. But great wealth often brings great problems: too many people crowding in, too much chance for corruption in government, and a widening gulf between the privileged few and the desperately poor majority.

Colombia

Colombia is the only nation in the Americas named for Christopher Columbus. Colombia sits in the northwestern corner of the continent. It is connected at the middle of its coastline to Panama, which is in Central America, by a narrow neck of land called the Isthmus of Panama. On one side of the isthmus, 710 miles (1,143 km) of Colombia's coastline touch the Caribbean Sea. On the other side of the isthmus, the Pacific Ocean washes onto about 580 miles (933 km) of Colombia's shores. To the east is Venezuela, to the southeast is Brazil, and to the south are both Peru and Ecuador.

The area of Colombia is 439,737 square miles (1,138,914 sq km), about the size of Texas and New Mexico combined. Its territory includes the Isla de San Andres, an island in the Caribbean Sea off the east coast of Nicaragua in Central America. About 4 million of Colombia's nearly 34 million people live in Bogotá, the capital, which is located on a plateau in the Andes at an altitude of 8,659 feet (2,639 m). Its name is derived from its Amerindian name, Bacata.

The Andes chain is divided into three ranges in Colombia. Bogotá's plateau is one of many plateaus

On the evening of November 13, 1985, Mount Ruiz blew its top. Sixteen-year-old Slaye Molina of the town of Armero remembered the disaster in a National Geographic *article. "... at 11:15 the mud came like a cloud. People screamed, 'The world is ending!' ... We rushed outside. ... The mud would catch up, and we would run faster. When we reached the hill, we saw Armero disappear in 15 minutes." This incredible disaster killed 23,000 people. The heat from the volcano melted only about 10 percent of the mountain's ice cap.*

The llanos (tropical grasslands) cover a large portion of Colombia. Beautiful birds, such as red ibis, spoonbills, and herons, live in the wetlands of this flat region.

A worker picking coffee cherries in fields on the middle slopes of Andean Cordillera Central. The shrubs thrive in the fertile volcanic soil.

in the Cordillera Oriental, the most eastern and the longest range.

The central range, Cordillera Central, has the highest peaks and many volcanoes, including the active Mount Ruiz, which is 17,716 feet (5,401 m) high. The lava from the volcanoes has made the land particularly fertile, ideal for growing coffee and, unfortunately, coca (the plant from which cocaine is made). Between the central range and the eastern range, Cordillera Oriental, is the Magdalena River valley, where much coffee is grown. The tallest peak in the range is Mount Huila, a volcano 18,865 feet (5,751 m) high.

The coastal range, Cordillera Occidental, is fairly low and parallels the coast. It has fewer people than the other ranges. Between this range and the central range lies the Cauca Valley, which is about 150 miles (242 km) long and an average of about 15 miles (24 km) wide. It is a major agricultural region.

Colombia is a land of great contrasts. The eastern two-thirds of the country feature grass-covered lowlands, called *llanos,* and tropical rain forests in the south near the equator. Here, some of Colombia's native people still follow the ancient ways of their ancestors, untouched by time.

Large river systems like the Magdalena and the Cauca make northwestern Colombia a productive agricultural region, where coffee and other crops thrive. The Cauca, a tributary of the Magdalena, drops steeply from the mountains, tumbling over rapids and through deep canyons.

Strangely, Colombia's highest mountain is not in the Andes proper. Cristóbal Colón is an isolated peak that abruptly rises 18,947 feet (5,777 m) near the Caribbean shore. Although not generally considered to be part of the Andes, some geologists say it is an extension of the Cordillera Central.

Ecuador

From Colombia, the Andes curve to the southwest into the Republic of Ecuador. The country is named for the equator, which crosses it. Compared to many South American countries, Ecuador is very small. It has an area covering only 109,484 square miles (283,561 sq km), about the size of the state of Colorado. Its population is over ten million, or about the same as Ohio's.

Nestled into northwestern South America, Ecuador is bordered by Colombia to the north, Peru to the east and south, and the Pacific Ocean to the west. The capital city of Quito in north-central Ecuador was once the northern capital of the Inca Empire. The Spaniards set up a government there in 1534.

Because of its rich soils and varied land features, Ecuador has long been a favorite site for scientists. British naturalist Charles Darwin made observations in the Galápagos Islands that contributed to his theories of the evolution of plants and animals. The first expedition to explore the Amazon River Basin, led by French geographer Charles-Marie de La Condamine, started in Ecuador in the 1700s.

The Andes Mountains dominate the landscape of the tiny country of Ecuador. The towering mountains dwarf many small cities.

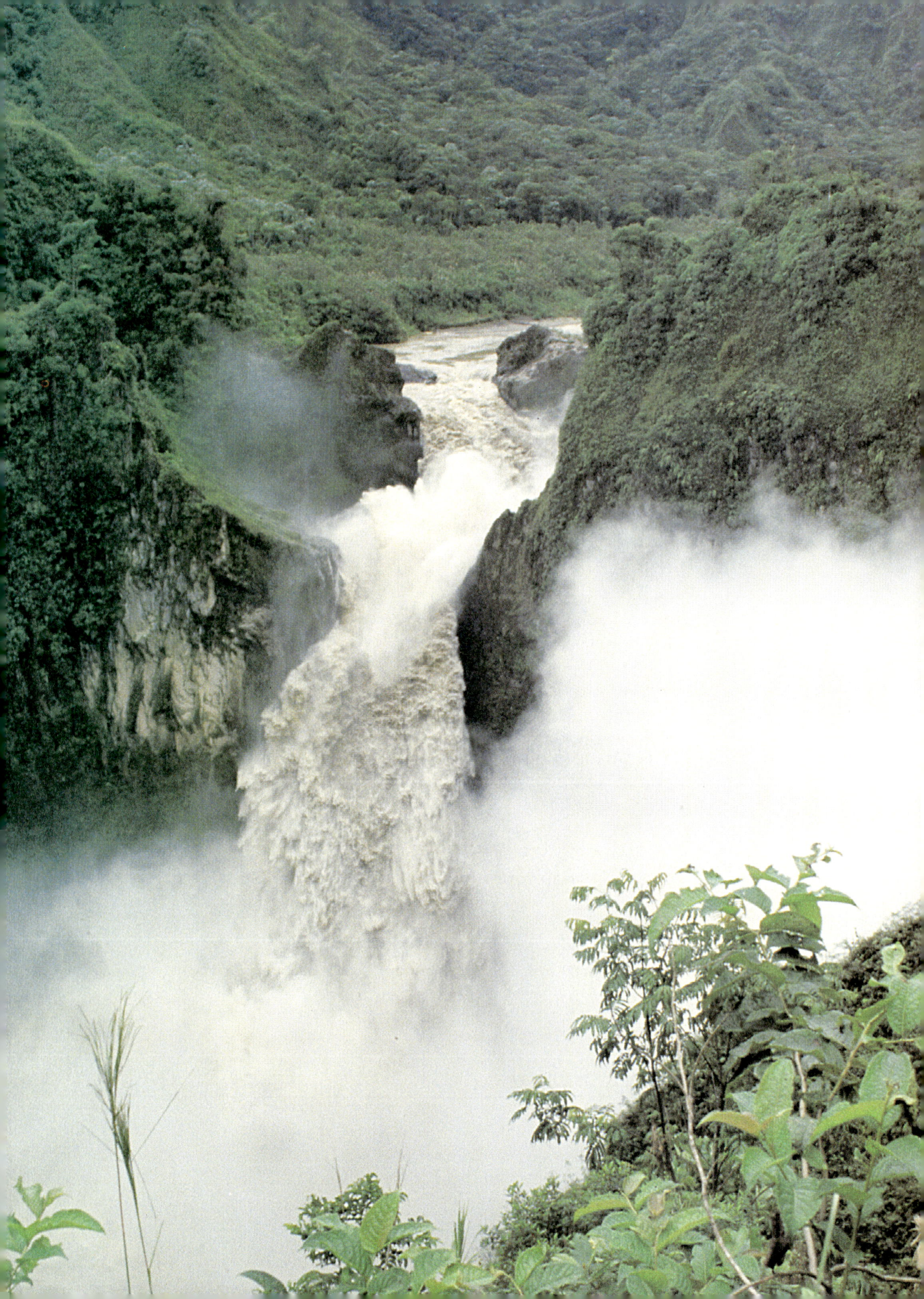

GALÁPAGOS: HOME OF THE GIANT TORTOISE

The Galápagos Islands, located 600 miles (966 km) west of the mainland, are part of Ecuador. They are famous for their unusual plant and animal life. This is the home of the giant tortoise, an animal that is believed to live longer than any other animal on Earth. Once widespread, these animals are now all but extinct. Some of the islands, which are mountains rising deep under the sea, are still active volcanoes.

Charles Darwin visited the islands in 1835. His study of geology told him that the islands were fairly new (probably only about 3 million years old). Also, he observed animals unlike those anywhere else on Earth. These things made him begin to wonder whether new species could develop—or evolve—to take advantage of new land. Up to that time, most people believed that all living things had been created at one time and had since remained unchanged.

No one claimed ownership of the Galápagos until Ecuador took them over in 1832. They are officially called the Archipiélago de Colón, named for Christopher Columbus. Today, the Galápagos, covering about 3,000 miles (4,830 sq km), are a wildlife sanctuary, a tourist attraction, and a scientist's delight. Ecuador, despite its economic problems, has made an important commitment to preserving the Galápagos.

The Andes are the main physical feature of Ecuador. They divide the land into three regions. Along the Pacific is the lowland coast, the Costa. In the east is the Oriente, also called the Amazon region, which extends to the border with Peru. The Andes run down the middle. In Ecuador they are known as the Sierra, the "highlands." The western and central Sierra form the highest and most continuous part of the chain in Ecuador. Between the two ranges, at an altitude of about 8,000 feet (2,400 m), lies a plateau that has been farmed by Amerindians since long before the Spanish came.

Many Ecuadorean mountains are volcanoes, including Chimborazo, the country's highest mountain, at 20,523 feet (6,269 m). It is no longer active, but Ecuador also has the highest active volcano in the world. It is Cotopaxi, southeast of Quito.

Even Cotopaxi is not alone. Mountain climber Loren McIntyre wrote in *National Geographic:* "From the icebound rim of Cotopaxi's steaming crater at 19,347 feet (5,898 m), I could see 12 other snow peaks, most of them volcanoes, lifting out of meadows and rain forests."

Sangay, located at 17,159 feet (5,231 m), has been an active volcano for centuries, but it is usually shrouded in clouds. Sangay is at the end of the active volcanic chain in the northern Andes.

South America's largest river system that flows

Located in the Andean cloud forest east of Quito, the Quijos River plunges dramatically, creating San Rafael Falls *(left).*

into the Pacific rises in the Andes. The Guayas River and its tributaries flow southwest into the Gulf of Guayaquil.

Ecuador is a mixed land of native Amerindians, white immigrants from Europe, mestizos, Africans, and settlers from China, Japan, Korea, and other countries. Amerindians comprise half the population, with most living in the valleys of the Andes.

The country now relies mainly on agricultural and mineral resources, exporting cacao (from which chocolate is made), bananas, shrimp, gold, and oil. It is also well known for making the misnamed Panama hat—the lightweight, natural-colored straw hat popular in the tropics.

Quito—officially Villa de San Francisco de Quito—is the oldest of all South American capital cities. At 9,000 feet (2,700 m) above sea level, it is also the second highest capital city in South America after La Paz, Bolivia. Its location high in the Andes Mountains gives Quito a climate somewhat like spring in Great Britain. The city existed even before the Incas made it part of their empire. It was refounded in 1534 by one of Francisco Pizarro's lieutenants, Sebastián de Benalcázar. Today, about 1.5 million people live in this urban area on the slopes of a volcano just south of the equator. The Machángara River winds through the old colonial section of the city.

Quito, Ecuador, is the second highest and the oldest capital city in South America.

Chapter Four

Central Andes
Peru • Bolivia

The central Andes continue southward into Peru, with the mountains still divided into three ranges—Cordillera Occidental, Central, and Oriental. By the time they reach the border, however, the central range has flattened out. The Occidental continues as part of Chile and the eastern, or Oriental, range is the only part that carries on into Bolivia. There it is called the Cordillera Real, meaning "Royal Range."

Peru

Directly south of Ecuador is the Republic of Peru. Covering an area of 496,225 square miles (1,285,216 sq km), it is the third largest country in South America, after Brazil and Argentina. Three times larger than California, Peru has about 22 million people—two-thirds of California's population. Peru's name comes from an Indian word that means "wealth."

Peru's neighbors are Ecuador and Colombia to the north, Bolivia and Brazil to the east, and Chile to the south. The capital city is Lima, located about halfway down the western coast.

Peru has three main land areas. In the west, the dry costa, or coastal region, lies between the Pacific Ocean and the slopes of the Andes. In the east is the *montaña*, the forested lowlands of the Amazon River Basin. Running down the center is the sierra, or the Peruvian Andes.

In northern Peru, the mountains are not as rugged as in most other areas of the Andes, rarely reaching more than 16,000 feet (4,877 m). But in central Peru, the range is quite a bit higher, with many snowcapped peaks. Here, east

33

The old colonial buildings of Arequipa were built with white volcanic rock called sillar.

of the city of Chimbote, is Mount Huascarán, the highest point in the Peruvian Andes at 22,205 feet (6,770 m). On May 31, 1970, Mount Huascarán exploded in a violent eruption that sent about 2 billion tons of earth, rock, and ice sliding down the glaciers into the valley below. The entire city of Yungay, with 18,000 people, was buried in an instant. Probably another 40,000 people in the vicinity died, too. It was the deadliest earthquake ever known in the Americas.

In southern Peru, the Andes form a high plateau called the Puna. A few peaks reach 21,000 feet (6,400 m). Near the city of Arequipa, the southern chain of volcanoes begins. Arequipa, founded in 1540, is often called "White City" because so many of its buildings are constructed of white volcanic rock. Like the other mountains surrounding the Pacific Ocean, the Peruvian Andes are young and prone to many earthquakes and shifting rocks.

Less than 100 miles (161 km) northeast of Arequipa and the same distance from the Pacific, a snowfield sits on top of a barren plateau on Mount Misti at an altitude of 19,101 feet (5,823 m). As the snow melts, it runs into the river, which drops a distance of 13,600 feet (4,145 m) in 310 miles (499 km).

THE FORESTS OF MANÚ

Southeastern Peru has a national park unlike any other in the world. It starts in the Amazon rain forest and then climbs the eastern slope of the Andes Mountains, to plateaus that reach an altitude of more than 12,000 feet (3,658 m). Two great rivers, the Manú and the Madre de Dios, flow through the park. With each change in altitude, the ecosystem changes, so that the park boasts an incredible variety of wildlife—from brilliant parrots and orchids to the rare spectacled bear and fierce mountain lions. At least 15 percent of the world's bird species live in the park. Its sixteen different ecosystems are home to a huge number of still unidentified species of both plants and animals.

Manú covers more land than Peru's other five national parks combined. Formed in June 1973, the national park is the central part of a UNESCO world biosphere reserve. Its great diversity of wildlife should be protected from development. However, oil drilling, a power plant, and other developments are endangering the Manú forests.

A number of small Amerindian groups live within the reserve just as their ancestors have lived for thousands of years. They live by hunting and fishing. But their life-style may be in the process of changing, too.

It then merges with other rivers flowing northward to form the mighty Amazon.

Peru is a land of extremes in weather. The desert along the western coast is very dry but not very hot. The northernmost point of Peru nearly touches the equator, while eastern Peru is hot and humid, and in the Andes, weather changes are common. When it is hot at sea level, it may be freezing on the snow-capped slopes.

Francisco Pizarro was not concerned with weather when he began exploring South America in 1524. He was searching for precious metals and other wealth for Spain—and for himself. He found silver in the region that became Peru. Fabulous wealth poured from deposits of silver and other precious metals. The ores were brought from the earth on the backs of the conquered native people.

Cuzco, Peru, was built on the ruins of the Inca capital. This street shows Spanish buildings constructed on top of an Inca stone wall.

Peru still has a wealth of mineral resources, such as gold, silver, copper, iron, lead, and zinc. It is not always easy to mine them, however, in this rugged terrain. Agriculture remains the most important industry.

Bolivia

Curving southeast at the Peruvian border, the Andes Mountains cross into Bolivia. This landlocked country is slightly smaller than Peru, covering 424,164 square miles (1,099,478 sq km). As the result of a war with Chile in the late nineteenth century, Bolivia lost its only Pacific coastline.

Bolivia has approximately seven million people, roughly the same number as the state of New Jersey. La Paz in west-central Bolivia is regarded

35

as the capital city. It is where the government meets. However, Sucre to the southwest is the official capital and home of the Supreme Court.

Bolivia is bordered by Chile and Peru to the west, Argentina to the south, Paraguay to the southeast, and Brazil to both the east and the north. Bolivia is named for Simón Bolívar, the Liberator.

Most of Bolivia is tropical forests, plains, swamps, and flooded bottomlands called the Oriente. In the extreme south is the Bolivian Chaco, part of the Gran Chaco, a name that comes from an Amerindian word meaning "hunting land." The Gran Chaco is a huge arid plain with only two rivers, few roads or rail lines, and very few people. No wonder—the Gran Chaco is a swamp in the rainy months and a desert the rest of the year.

However, in 1932, Bolivia and Paraguay fought a full-scale war over the Chaco. The Chaco War lasted three years, and 100,000 Bolivians died. Bolivia also lost more territory than Paraguay had wanted in the first place.

The Andes Mountains cover about one-third of Bolivia in the southwest, but this is the most devel-

Andean mountain peaks and glaciers can be viewed from the air when approaching the La Paz, Bolivia, airport.

oped and densely populated region. It is one of the highest places in the world where people live.

Two great Andean ranges run through Bolivia side by side. They are the Cordillera Occidental along the Chilean border and the Cordillera Oriental to the east. The Occidental is a lively area of active volcanoes. It has the highest point in Bolivia, Mount Sajama, at 21,463 feet (6,542 m). However, the Oriental has the Cordillera Real, or Royal Range, near La Paz, a spectacular, 200-mile (322-km) line of snowcapped peaks reaching an average of 18,000 feet (5,486 m).

Between these two ranges, nature has carved the widest part of the Andes, the broad plateau called the Altiplano. This "high plain" is one of the largest interior drainage basins, or watersheds, in the world—500 miles (805 km) long and 80 miles (129 km) wide, with no outlet to the ocean. To the east is Potosí, founded in 1545 when the Spaniards discovered the largest known deposits of silver in the world. Potosí was the largest city in the Americas in the middle of the seventeenth century, with about 160,000 people. Today it has a population of a little over 100,000.

Lake Titicaca, on the Peru-Bolivia border, is located on the Altiplano. When the last Ice Age was ending, about 10,000 years ago, the Altiplano was covered with two massive lakes. As the land dried

Alpacas, relatives of llamas, graze on the grasses of the Altiplano in Bolivia. Alpacas are bred more for their warm wool than for use as pack animals.

Sheep have become a mainstay of the native people, even though they cannot be raised at as high an elevation as alpacas. This woman watches her sheep on the Altiplano.

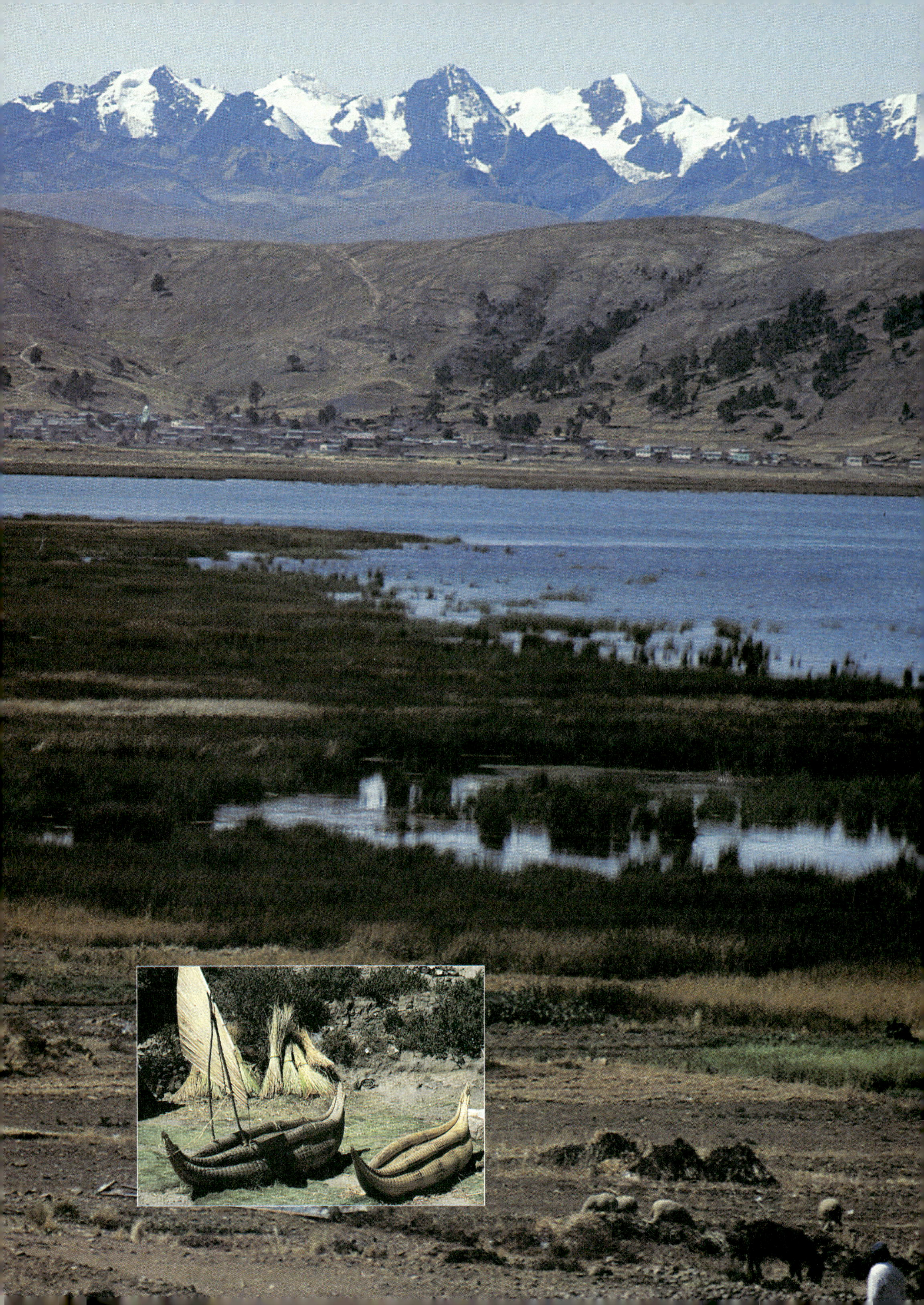

Lake Titicaca *(left)*, **on the border between Peru and Bolivia, is the world's highest inland lake that can accommodate large boats. The Aymara people who use the lake sail small boats made of balsa** *(inset left)*, **with sails made of tortora reeds.**

out, the northern lake became Lake Titicaca. The southern lake dried up, leaving a huge expanse of mud and salt flats.

Many people live on the 41 islands in Lake Titicaca. The biggest is the Isla del Sol, or Isle of the Sun. The Incas believed that the founders of their empire, sent by the sun god, arrived on Earth there.

At least 25 rivers feed their water into Lake Titicaca. But only one small river flows out at the south end—the Desaguadero River. All the other water evaporates in the sun and the wind. Most lakes that evaporate a lot of water gradually turn very salty, but so much fresh water pours into Lake Titicaca that it remains usable.

The Desaguadero River has long flowed into the only other large lake on the Altiplano, Lake Poopó in central Bolivia. Lake Titicaca is quite deep, averaging more than 400 feet (122 m), but Lake Poopó is little more than a huge puddle, about 8 to 10 feet (2.4 to 3 m) deep.

The Aymara people live on the high plateau near Lake Titicaca. Largely isolated from the main Bolivian society, they exist by growing a few crops on their poor land and by raising some livestock. Thousands of their ancestors died in the copper mines, which flourished until the eighteenth century. Many Aymara people have migrated to overcrowded cities in search of a better life.

The richest veins of the famed tin mines of South America also ran out long ago, and tin mining is no longer nearly as important as it once was. Nevertheless, tin mining is still part of the nation's economy. The ore, usually found in the high mountains, is costly, difficult, and dangerous to remove.

Aymara people dance along the lake shore in a Catholic feast day celebration.

39

Bolivia's most important industry still is mining. These native women of the Altiplano work in a zinc mine in Negra.

Today, other minerals, such as lead and zinc, also have to be mined in the area if the mining of tin ore is to be profitable.

Like many South American countries, Bolivia's people are made up of three groups—descendants of the Spaniards, mestizos of mixed Amerindian and Spanish ancestry, and Amerindians—most of whom speak Quechua, the language of the Incas. There are few immigrants, though in the 1960s a small group of Japanese and Okinawan farmers successfully settled on the land.

In 1900, about one-tenth of all Bolivians lived in rural areas. Today about one-half of the people live in the cities, and more than 1.5 million live in the largest city—La Paz.

Located about 42 miles (68 km) from Lake Titicaca, La Paz sits high in the Andes, the highest capital city in the world at about 12,000 feet (3,658 m). Unless you are a native of the region, just walking around in La Paz can make you tired. That's because the air at such a high altitude is so thin that not enough oxygen gets into the lungs.

The city La Paz, whose name means "peace" in Spanish, was founded in 1548. The snowcapped peaks of the spectacular Cordillera Real look down on steep, narrow streets, skyscrapers, red-tile roofs, and highland Amerindians in colorful native dress. The city has grown so quickly in the past few years that houses are climbing right up the canyon walls at the foot of Mount Illimani.

La Paz *(right)*, the highest major city in the world, has spread through its valley toward the nearby peak of Mount Illimani.

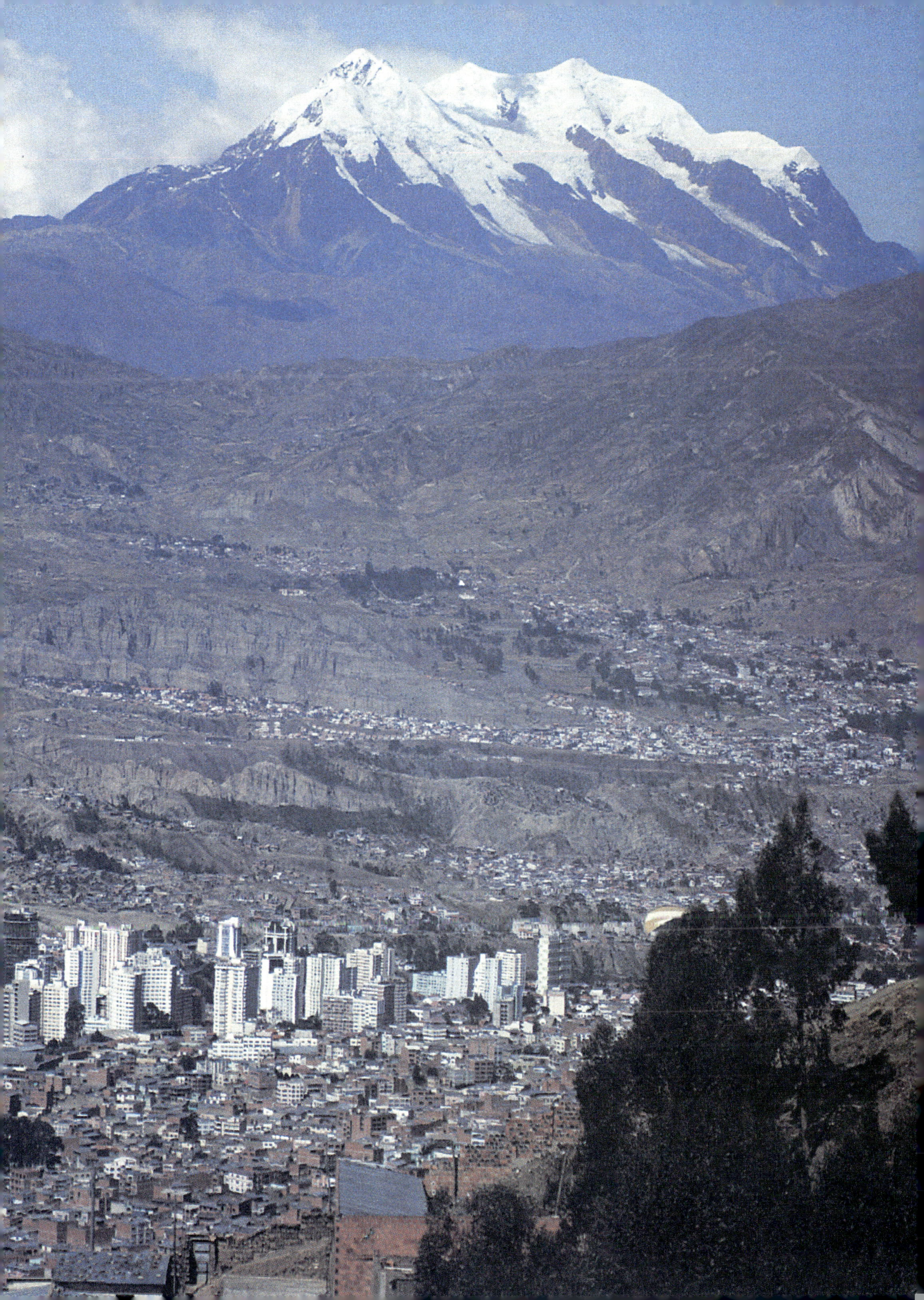

Chapter Five

Southern Andes
Chile • Argentina

The southern Andes Mountains run through just two nations. Chile, located in the west, is very long and narrow. Argentina, in the east, is much larger and wider.

Chile

South of Peru and Bolivia is possibly the world's most strangely shaped country—the Republic of Chile. A Chilean writer once called this long stringbean of a land *loca*, meaning "crazy," because it has so many different landscapes and so many different climates.

Chile is 2,650 miles (4,265 km) long. If you placed a map of Chile over a map of North America, Chile would stretch from southern Alaska to the end of southern Mexico. Yet, from east to west it averages only 110 miles (177 km) wide! That's about the distance from New York City to Boston, Massachusetts. At its narrowest, Chile is 56 miles (90 km) wide, barely enough space for a few good mountains!

Chile is larger than the state of Texas, with an area of 292,135 square miles (756,626 sq km). Its population is 13 million, about the same as the number of people living in Florida.

All of western Chile borders the Pacific Ocean. Most of its elongated eastern border is shared with Argentina. Peru and Bolivia share the northern and northeastern border. Within this narrow strip of a nation, three different landforms run side by side down

Active Villarica volcano is located near the town of Pucón, Chile. This popular tourist town boasts a beach of black sand.

The coastline outside the port of Antofagasta is located in Chile's northern desert region. A Bolivian silver refinery used to be located in this city.

its length. Along the Pacific are the low coastal ranges, not more than 7,000 feet (2,100 m) high and not regarded as part of the Andes.

Along the eastern border are the Chilean Andes. This is the highest part of the mountain system, with spectacularly snowcapped peaks, steep slopes, and deep valleys. In the north, these peaks rise between 16,000 and 19,000 feet (4,877 and 5,791 m). Most of the higher ones are dead volcanoes. However, many of Chile's volcanoes are very much alive. Chileans are well aware that they could erupt at any moment. And some of them do. In addition to volcanic eruptions, the shifting mountains produce earthquakes. Terrible quakes in 1960 and 1985 left thousands of people homeless.

The northern part of Chile (and the southern part of Bolivia) is a desert region called the Atacama. It covers a plateau about 12,000 feet (3,658 m) high. Some scientists say the Atacama is the driest place on Earth—it has had periods of more than twenty years when not a single drop of rain fell. The soil is so salty that, even with rain, plants won't grow there. There are some valleys in the desert, however, where underground springs provide water for some shrubs and low, coarse plants to grow. On the northern edge of the Atacama is Mount Ojos del Salado, the highest mountain in Chile at 22,572 feet (6,882 m).

South of the Atacama is a region of semidesert,

43

"One version of the origin of Chile is that at the Creation, after God had finished His Labors, as a final task, He asked the angels to sweep some leftover pieces behind a high wall in an out-of-the-way corner of the globe; the wall was the Andes, and the leftovers, a motley assortment, formed Chile."

— South American geographer Arthur Morris

leading to a beautiful and productive fertile valley. In this part of Chile, known as the Central Valley, the soil is good, water is plentiful, and temperatures are moderate. Not surprisingly, this is where most of Chile's people live. It is also Chile's major agricultural region, where even steep slopes are planted whenever possible.

Chile's people are mainly mixed European and Amerindian. The descendants of the old Spanish aristocracy, however, dominate the country as they have for centuries. A small number of English, Italian, French, and German immigrants have become part of the population. There are few Africans because plantations did not develop in Chile during the colonial period, and so few slaves were brought into the country.

The city of Santiago, with a population of about five million, sits on the Mapocho River with a view of the high Andes to the east. Santiago became the capital of the country in 1818.

The forests of Chile, located in the central and southern parts of the country, were virtually wiped out before the 1970s by farmers using the slash-

The capital of Santiago lies in the central region of Chile. Almost 70 percent of the country's people live in this area of frequent earthquakes.

This Chilean land was completely eroded by wind and rain after moisture-holding trees were cut down.

and-burn technique to clear the land and by the timber industry endlessly cutting trees without replacing them. Without tree roots to hold the soil in place, mile after mile of land was devastated. Most of the topsoil was carried away by rainwater and dumped into the seas and rivers. There was so little fertile soil left that many farmers were unable to grow even enough food to feed their families.

In 1973, however, a law was passed that called for reforesting the land. The government paid for most of the seedlings and fully supported anything necessary to make trees grow again. By 1986, Chile had the largest human-planted forest in the world. Almost half of the Chilean land is now forested.

Most of the new forest was planted with an imported tree called the Monterey, or radiata, pine, which comes from North America. The conditions where the trees grow are virtually identical to those of the southwestern United States where the tree originated. The tree is officially called *pino distinguido*, or "distinguished pine," because of its importance to the Chilean forest products industry.

South of the forests is Patagonia, a cold, rugged mountainous land. This region gradually breaks into numerous islands, both large and small.

Most of Chile's rivers begin in the Andes and quickly flow downhill, creating many rapids. A group of rafters on the Trancura River enjoys the rough ride.

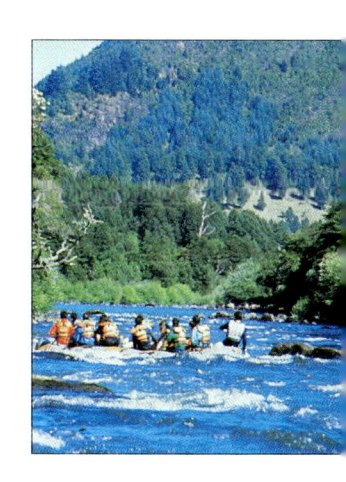

Argentina

Chile shares both the Andes and a long border with the Republic of Argentina. These countries occupy almost all of southern South America. Argentina is the continent's second largest nation, after Brazil, and the eighth largest in the world. With an area over 1 million square miles (2.8 million sq km), it is four times larger than Texas and it has almost twice as many people—about 32 million. Its name is derived from the Latin word *argentum*, meaning "silver." The Spanish were looking for silver when they explored the Atlantic coast of South America in the sixteenth century. They had heard stories about the "enchanted City of the Caesars," a legend like the Eldorado tale of gold in North America.

In addition to Chile to the south and west, Argentina shares boundaries with Bolivia and Paraguay on the north, and Brazil, Uruguay, and the Atlantic Ocean on the east.

Northern Argentina contains the hot lowlands called the Gran Chaco. To the south is the huge, flat, grass-covered Pampas, a Quechua word meaning "flat surface." In the extreme south, Argentina and Chile share the broad plateau of Patagonia.

Patagonia is a barren tableland of about 300,000 square miles (777,630 sq km) in southern South America between the Andes and the Atlantic Ocean. Part of it is in Chile and part in Argentina. Perhaps its windy climate is the reason that it was practically unexplored until the second half of the nineteenth century. In fact, the native peoples advise visitors who wish to see Patagonia, "just stand still and it will all blow past you."

The world's southernmost city is Ushuaia, the capital of Tierra del Fuego. It is closer to the South Pole than to the northern end of Argentina. To attract people to this remote land, the government of Argentina reduced taxes for companies who built factories there. The city is now a major producer of color TV sets. In 1992, the city built an airport big enough to handle jumbo jets.

There are very few trees in Patagonia. The wind is too strong for many trees to grow.

Guira cuckoos are one of many bird species that live in Patagonia.

The Andes Mountains dominate almost the entire western border of Argentina for some 2,300 miles (3,701 km). Here, the mountain chain is only 200 miles (322 km) wide, narrower than anywhere else on the continent.

South America's highest mountain, Aconcagua, rises 22,831 feet (6,959 m) in northwest Argentina. Aconcagua is a major challenge to mountain climbers—not because it's so high but because the winds are so fierce. It was first climbed in 1897, by Swiss mountaineer Matthias Zurbriggen. Many climbers who did not believe that the winds could make the climb so difficult are buried in a cemetery on the mountain.

Argentina has many other peaks over 21,000 feet (6,400 m). Some are volcanic. Most of the country is in the temperate zone, so its climate is milder

The lesser rhea, a tall, flightless bird with three toes on each foot, is found in the Pampas of Argentina.

than that of its northern neighbors nearer to the equator. However, many of the Andean peaks are capped by ice or snow year-round.

The Río de la Plata is formed by the meeting of the Uruguay and Paraná rivers. In northeastern Argentina at the border with Brazil, near where the Iguazú River joins the Paraná, is the horseshoe-shaped Iguazú Falls. This spectacular waterfall is almost three times the width of Niagara Falls in North America! The river plunges over some 275 separate waterfalls around the horseshoe-shaped curve of land. A curtain of mist from the falling water rises 500 feet (152 m) in the air, creating an endless string of rainbows in the sunshine. Both Argentina and Brazil have national parks around the falls. Brazil calls the waterfall Iguaçu Falls.

The Spanish first explored Argentina in 1516 when Juan Díaz de Solís discovered the Río de la Plata. Today, most of the people are of European descent. Large numbers immigrated from Spain and Italy. Amerindians and other minorities make up a small percentage of Argentina's population. Some of them have been absorbed into the white culture; many others live in poor rural areas.

For decades, the nation of Argentina, and all the countries of the Andes—including the people, the animal and plant life, and the land itself—have

THE GAUCHOS OF THE PAMPAS

The Pampas of Argentina is probably best known for being the home of the famous and colorful horsemen called gauchos. They once roamed the Pampas, rounding up herds of escaped horses and cattle. Gauchos were skilled in the use of the bola, a device made of leather cords attached to three iron balls or stones. When thrown, the bola wraps around the legs of running cattle, bringing them down. The free-spirited gauchos wore long pleated pants gathered at the ankles over high leather boots. This clothing is still worn by many cowhands who work the Pampas today. The gauchos in this picture are working to control the cattle at a livestock auction.

48

seemed to be protected by the nearly impenetrable mountains. But many parts of the world today suffer from pollution and wasting of resources. Could this be true of the Andes? Is this massive, rugged mountain range and its wildlife in danger?

Spectacular Iguazú Falls is three times wider than Niagara Falls. Iguazú means "great river."

A lone guanaco (related to llamas and alpacas) stands on the plain below the rugged Chilean Andes.

Chapter Six

Are the Andes in Danger?

The Cordillera of the Andes, stretching down the west coast of South America in a long, broken chain, looks solid and safe. The mountains create an unchanging wall of protection. Or do they?

Until well into the twentieth century, it seemed to many scientists that the Andes could not suffer the environmental problems that threaten other areas. Today, they are not so sure. Part of the uncertainty is just because the Andes are the Andes. They are so high and so long. Parts of them are so rugged, so wild, and so remote that it is impossible to know for sure what is happening everywhere. But there are some troubling signs.

Unchecked erosion, pollution, misuse of land, destruction of forests, poor mining practices—all these can destroy the delicate ecological balance in a mountainous terrain like the Andes.

Endangered Land

Only about ten percent of the entire continent of South America is actually covered with fertile soil. Erosion is always at work, exposing the underlying rock. Once-fertile wheat fields on some slopes of the Andes are no longer productive. They have been abandoned, leaving them open to more erosion. Mountain forests have been cleared for farming and for grazing cattle. Animal herders have destroyed acres of grasslands in the high Andes of Venezuela.

Part of the problem is that many people who live in the high remote Andes farm and tend cattle just as their ancestors did. Even though the cattle produce nutrient-filled dung, the farmers dry the dung and use it as fuel instead of as fertilizer for their land. They do not want to change their ways. It is often difficult for many governments of South American countries to convince these Andean people who live at high altitudes that what has been done for centuries may now be harming their mountain land.

Most of the ecological problems in the Andes can be traced to human misuse of the land. People have destroyed forests and grasslands with little thought for the future. Trees are cut for timber and to clear land for mineral mining and for agriculture. As

People of the Andean region use three million tons of wood each year, most of it cut by the rural poor. The U.N. Food and Agriculture Organization started a reforestation program in Peru in the 1980s to help solve this problem.

DRUGS THREATEN THE ENVIRONMENT

Illegal drugs threaten the lives of people all over the world. But Andean farmers, such as the one in this picture, make their living cultivating coca leaves, from which cocaine is made. Chewing coca leaves for medicinal purposes has been a part of the culture of Andean native people for hundreds of years. In the 1960s, however, as the international demand for illegal cocaine mushroomed in North America and Europe, coca became the most profitable crop for farmers to grow. Today, almost $5 billion worth of cocaine leaves Bolivia alone each year. Much of Peru's scarce farming land—only about 3 percent of the nation's land is arable—is cleared illegally for growing coca, leaving behind too many people on too little usable land. Coca growing and processing also threaten the environment. The chemical process used in making cocaine ruins the land. Drug traffickers dump chemicals into waterways, poisoning the water and the soil. The cocaine is smuggled to the big Colombian drug cartels in the cities of Calí and Medellín, from which it is shipped all over the world.

Argentina's forests are harvested for lumber, firewood, and charcoal.

more and more of this land is eroded, the damaged soil can no longer produce enough food to feed the poor who work the land. As a result, people push ever deeper into wilderness lands in search of places to farm. More forests are destroyed, more land is eroded, and the process goes on and on.

Another problem is energy exploration and exploitation. Getting oil out of the ground is easy compared to getting it over the Andes to the Pacific coast. In Ecuador, for example, the oil industry faced the awesome task of laying pipelines up and over the forbidding peaks of the Ecuadorian Andes. Today, the oil flows from Amazon Basin wells deep in the eastern jungles of Ecuador, over the Andes,

Oil exploration and production in the Amazon region of eastern Ecuador threatens not only the rain forest, but also the ecology of the Andes, since the oil must be piped over the rugged Andes to coastal ports.

and across the Costa region to the sea. Some ecologists worry that the oil pipelines will eventually damage the delicate ecology of both the Costa and the Andes.

Although most South American governments realize the threat to the Andes and to the rest of the continent, they have not found a successful formula for the protection of the land. Ecologists warn that unless reform comes soon, much of the beautiful wilderness that is the Andes Mountains will be gone forever.

Endangered Wildlife

The Andes teem with an amazing variety of plant and animal life. South America has more species of birds than any other continent. But there isn't necessarily safety in numbers. Even in areas once considered too remote for hunting, animal habitats have been destroyed. As a result, many animal populations are dwindling in number and some may be threatened with extinction.

Scientists are keeping a particularly watchful eye on the Andean condor, the largest of all flying birds. The 10-foot (3-m) wingspan on this huge vulture makes it slightly larger than the next largest, the California condor. The Andean, or South American, condor weighs about 22 pounds (10 kg). It is black with a white ruff and a bare pinkish head. It ranges from the Pacific coast of South America to the high Andes, feeding on dead animals and fish. It breeds only every other year, laying two white eggs at altitudes above 10,000 feet (3,048 m). The wild condors still fly the Andes, but their California relatives are in danger of extinction. Today the Andean condors are part of a very important experiment.

Rather than take a chance on losing the eggs or young of the very few remaining California condors, biologists decided to try their population-rebuilding techniques using Andean condors. In 1980, eleven young Andean condors that had been bred and raised in captivity were released in Peru. By 1985, most of them had learned survival skills from wild birds and were thriving in the wild.

The pudu is the smallest American deer. Limited numbers of this mammal are found in Bolivia and Chile.

The range of the Andean condor extends from high in the Andes Mountains to the Pacific coast of South America. These magnificent birds make their nests at altitudes above 10,000 feet (3,000 m).

The population of the endangered huemul deer is only several thousand. Much of their range in Patagonia has been fenced off by cattle ranchers.

Some biologists have thought that because there were no longer California condors in the wild, there was no point in trying to rebuild the population. But other naturalists decided it was possible to rebuild a colony using Andean condors to help train the young captive-bred Californian birds to survive. Andean condors were released both in California and Colombia, in the hope of learning enough about their behavior to help California condors make a comeback.

Another animal in danger is the small deer called the huemul. It once roamed the plateau of Patagonia in southern Chile and Argentina in huge numbers. Today there are only a few thousand of these small deer. Much of the huemul's grazing land was taken away when ranchers came to the region. In the 1940s and 1950s, thousands of miles of forests were burned to make pasture for cattle. The huemul's habitat is shrinking daily.

Conservation in Andean lands is not yet as well organized as it is on other continents. Until it is, this unique region is in ecological danger.

National Parks

A country's record on conservation may be judged partly by its national parks and animal reserves. There are not many such places in the Andes, but some nations work hard to protect plant and animal life.

Tiny Ecuador, for instance, has set aside about 25 million acres (10 million ha) of its land into national parks and nature preserves. Two of them surround the volcanoes of Cotopaxi and Sangay. The country's most famous reserve is the Galápagos Islands National Park created in 1935. But the fragile ecology of these remote and unique islands is threatened today from four sources: poachers who prey on the famous tortoises found on the Galápagos, unregulated clearing of the land, domestic animals that were introduced by the first settlers, and tourists.

Bolivia has six national parks that cover more than 6 million acres (2.4 million ha). Bellavista National Park and Isiboro-Securé National Park are located east of La Paz.

Venezuela has seven national parks. The Henri Pittier National Park, named for a French-Swiss

The marine iguana is one of the unique species found only in the Galápagos Islands.

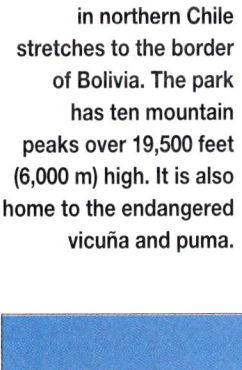

Lauca National Park in northern Chile stretches to the border of Bolivia. The park has ten mountain peaks over 19,500 feet (6,000 m) high. It is also home to the endangered vicuña and puma.

55

SAVING BY SHAVING

High in the Andes lives the vicuña, a small, furry relative of the Amerindians' pack animal, the llama. "Furry" is the important word, because its fine soft fur, the color of caramel, has been highly valued for weaving wonderfully soft fabrics. In ancient days, only Inca rulers wore clothing made of vicuña fur. It was collected in a great royal hunt during which animals were rounded up. Then laborers shaved the very softest fur from the animals' backs. The vicuña were then released. But after the Spanish conquest, people who wanted the fur found it easier just to shoot the vicuña.

In Peru, it is estimated that the nation's 400,000 vicuñas were reduced to fewer than 5,000 between 1950 and 1960. Conservationists all over the world urged that the animals be protected, and gradually the countries where the vicuña live have established national parks. Unfortunately, that did not stop the poaching, so naturalists looked for a better solution.

Peru is trying one such experiment. It has gone back to the old Inca method of shearing the animals like sheep, so that today vicuña wool is sold on world markets. Now that the wool is available, a lot of the illegal poaching is not as profitable, and the herds are beginning to build up once again.

The Incas gave the puma its name. This graceful cat is killed for its beautiful coat.

naturalist, is part of the Cordillera de la Costa and protects more than 500 species of birds.

Chile has put about 20 million of its acres (8.1 million ha) into national parks. Two of these parks were developed especially to protect endangered animals. The Lauca National Park protects Chile's dwindling vicuña herds. The wild vicuña is related to the llama, the workhorse of the Andes.

In the far south of Chile, in Patagonia, under the lofty shadows of the Andes, is the Torres del Paine National Park. Here roams the elusive, magnificent animal that is known as the Patagonia puma. These fleet-footed cats can grow to 150 or more pounds (68 kg) of muscle, claws, and teeth! Pumas—known elsewhere as cougars, panthers, or mountain lions—were once in danger of extinction in Chile, especially from sheepherders because pumas have a fondness for sheep. However, since 1980 it has been illegal in Chile to kill these big cats, making this country a pioneer in South American wildlife rights.

Unfortunately, Chile has not been as successful with plant life. Of the country's four national reserves, Juan Fernandez National Park, created in 1935, is the most threatened. This tourist attraction of three islands off the coast is the site of the true story behind the famous book *Robinson Crusoe* by Daniel Defoe. The park has many spectacular and unique flora, which, unfortunately, are in danger of extinction. There are very few government regulations to protect the area. Forests are destroyed, sheep farming is encouraged, land is cleared for settlement, and domestic animals are introduced with little thought to their impact on the ecology. Some scientists fear that Juan Fernandez National Park will soon be destroyed.

Five of Argentina's 17 national parks are in the Andes. One of them—Los Glacieres in Patagonia—is on the United Nations' World Heritage List of natural sites to be preserved.

Argentina has been a pioneer in wildlife protection. The Nahuel Huapí National Park was established in 1903 to preserve part of the Andes. It features beech forests, glaciers, and many animals. But even in Argentina, trouble threatens. The beautiful cypress trees called *alerce* grow in only one place in the world—a narrow strip of the Patagonian Andes known as Los Alerces National Park. Even though it is illegal to cut the tree, many are destroyed yearly. Now the whole park may be threatened by plans to build a huge dam that would flood certain parts of the reserve.

Argentina's Los Alerces National Park was named after the beautiful cypress trees called *alerce* that grow there.

Urban Problems in the Andes

The land of the Andes has remained fairly stable through the centuries. Today it seems that so much of it is changing. Why?

The main reason is people. The population of South America is increasing at an alarming rate. As in countries all over the world, rural people are moving into already overcrowded urban centers seeking a better way of life. It is difficult to find.

Lima, Peru, is an example. About one-third of Peru's nearly 22 million people live in and around its capital city. That is one of the country's major problems—too many people in too little space. Small wonder that Lima's popular nickname is *El Pulpo*—"the Octopus." The city sprawls out in all directions, a small oasis in a coastal desert overshadowed by the Andes.

For many years, the mountains kept down traffic from the east. Lima and its port city of Callao were Peru's only contacts with the outside world. But railroads and automobiles opened up the country and brought thousands of rural people into the capital city.

Lima was not prepared for the invasion. It still isn't. The city has only one freeway and an outdated mass transportation system. It does, however, have all the problems of most twentieth-century urban centers: it is noisy, polluted, dirty, and overcrowded. There is so much congestion and pollution from automobiles and buses that it is said the citizens of Lima can taste the air.

These two Peruvian children will probably live in poverty their entire lives.

Many poor people from rural Andean towns in Peru leave for a better life in Lima and other urban areas. What they find, however, is more poverty and a life of desperation as they become the urban poor.

58

Lima is unbearably hot and humid in the summer months. Wealthy people have homes on the coast to escape the heat, but the growing numbers of people who live in slums or poor neighborhoods are not so fortunate. During colonial days, many spacious mansions were built in what is now the inner city. Today most of these old homes have been divided to hold as many as fifty families. Peruvians who have come from all over the country seeking a better life rarely find it in these inner-city slums. For most, their dreams of a good sewage system and a steady job are still unrealized.

As more people crowd into Lima and the outskirts, they use more land and more of the land's natural resources. Few people give much thought to conserving the natural environment and preserving the future. Will the pollution of crowded urban centers such as Lima eventually harm the delicate balance of nature on the slopes of the Andes? Will more forests be destroyed on mountain slopes, leaving more land open to erosion and more animals of the Andes in danger? No one knows for certain. But many people are concerned.

Many Colombian children of urban Bogotá sift through trash searching for things they can use or sell.

Protecting the Andes

In June 1992, the United Nations sponsored a huge international conference in Brazil called the Earth Summit. This meeting was concerned with all the places on Earth where human activity affects the environment. The Andes and other highly sensitive areas were very high on the agenda. The conference secretary-general told attendees, "We can change course. We can improve living standards . . . we can better manage and protect the ecosystem."

The Earth Summit and other groups want better mining and farming practices, more effective hunting laws, and more protection for animals. They also want a better life for the people who live in overcrowded cities like Lima and in the high peaks of the Andes.

Few people live higher in the world than the Amerindians of Ausangate, a nearly 21,000-foot (6,400-m) peak in the Peruvian Andes. It would be hard to imagine a life more different from the crowded streets of Lima or more remote. Children walk through a treeless world more than 15,000 feet (4,572 m) above sea level. For most people, just

59

breathing at that elevation is hard work. But the people who were born there travel in the mountains with ease. Families live in stone houses with grass roofs. They carry their water supply from a nearby lake. They haul great loads of llama dung back to their homes for fuel. They must use a lot of fuel—in the thin air it takes hours just to boil potatoes, the people's main food.

The all-important llama herds of the Ausangate people also supply them with food and clothing. The women wear as many as a dozen wool petticoats at a time to keep warm in this rarified atmosphere. When "the sun swims under the Earth," as the Inca used to say, the mountain air is freezing. The people stir the fire embers and crawl into warm clothing made from alpaca wool.

These dwellers of the high Andes live as their ancestors have lived for centuries. The mountains that surround them look as they always have . . . at least for now. But will pollution from the overcrowded urban centers one day threaten their way of life? Will the wasting of natural resources on these mountains change the delicate balance of nature?

We know that the Cordillera of the Andes is one of Earth's special places—a spectacular mountain system that is massive, primitive, frightening, and beautiful. What we don't know is if, or by how much, pollution and misuse of Earth's resources threaten the land of the Andes.

The white-tipped tapir of the wooded mountainsides. Tapirs are large, piglike hoofed mammals that walk the countryside with their snouts to the ground, looking for buds and fruits.

The beauty of Los Alerces National Park in Argentina (right) reminds visitors why the Andes Mountains must be protected.

Llamas are reliable pack animals for the natives of the Andes. They also provide food and fiber for clothing.

GLOSSARY

archipelago – a chain of scattered islands.

ecology – a branch of science that deals with the relationship between organisms and their environment.

ecosystem – a natural community of plants and animals and its environment, which function as one unit.

erosion – the slow wearing away of soil or rock, caused by the actions of wind, water, or glacial ice.

flash flood – a local flood, usually of short duration, resulting from heavy rain in the area.

glacier – a large body of permanent ice that moves slowly down a slope.

immigrants – people who come to a country to take up permanent residence.

lava – fluid rock that flows from a volcano.

mestizo – a person of mixed European and Native South American ancestry.

occidental – western.

oriental – eastern.

plain – a large area of level, generally treeless land.

plateau – a large area of level, generally treeless land that is higher than adjacent land at least on one side.

rain forest – woodland, especially in a tropical area, that usually has 100 or more inches of rain yearly.

volcano – a hill or mountain with an opening at the top, which spews lava and steam periodically. A hill or mountain composed of this material.

FOR MORE INFORMATION

Americas magazine.
Caistor, Nick. *Argentina*. World in View series. Austin, Tex.: Raintree Steck-Vaughn, 1991.
Central and South America. Lands and People series, Vol. 6. Danbury, Conn.: Grolier, 1991.
Collinson, Allan. *Mountains*. Ecology Watch series. New York: Dillon Press, 1992.
Dineen, Jacqueline. *Volcanoes*. New York: Watts, 1991.
Dwyer, Christopher. *Chile*. Places and People of the World series. New York: Chelsea, 1989.
Fox, Jeffrey. *Land and People of Argentina*. Philadelphia: Lippincott, 1990.
Jacobsen, Karen. *Chile*. Chicago: Childrens Press, 1991.
Lauber, Patricia. *Volcanoes and Earthquakes*. New York: Scholastic, 1991 (pap.).
Lepthien, Emilie U. *Ecuador*. Chicago: Childrens Press, 1986.
Morrison, Marion. *Ecuador, Peru, and Bolivia*. World in View series. Austin, Tex.: Raintree Steck-Vaughn, 1992.
National Geographic magazine.
Odijk, Pamela. *Incas*. Morristown, N.J.: Silver Burdett, 1990.
Smith, Anthony. *Exploration of the Amazon*. New York: Viking, 1990.
Stewart, Gail B. *Colombia*. New York: Macmillan, 1991.

INDEX

Aconcagua 6, 7, 8, 46, 47
Africa 14, 18, 27, 44
agriculture 14, 22, 27, 28, 32, 35, 44
Alaska 16, 42
alerce 57
alpaca 37, 50, 60
Altiplano 33, 36, 37, 40
altitude 40
Amazon River 8, 12, 14, 29, 33, 35
Amerindians 14, 18, 20, 27, 31, 32, 34, 36, 40, 44, 48, 56, 59
ancestors 18, 51, 60
anchovies 11
Andean condor 53–54
Andes 4, 6, 7, 9, 11, 12, 14, 15, 16, 17, 18, 19, 21–22, 25, 26, 27–29, 31–32, 33–34, 35, 40, 42, 43, 44, 45, 46, 47, 48–49, 50, 51, 53, 55, 58, 59–60
Andes de Patagonia 8, 42
animals 21–22, 29, 37, 48–49 53, 55, 57, 59
Antarctic Ocean 8, 9
Antarctica 14
Antofagasta, Chile 8, 42, 43
Appalachian Mountains 6, 7
Apurímac River 33
Araucanians 20
archipelago 4
Archipiélago de Colón 31
Arequipa, Peru 8, 33, 34
Argentina 4, 6, 8, 14, 15, 17, 24, 36, 42, 46–49, 49, 54, 60
argentum 46
Armero, Venezuela 27
ash 6
Asunción, Paraguay 8
Atacama Desert 42, 43
Atlantic Ocean 8, 12, 14, 25, 42, 46
Aucanquilcha Volcano 19, 42
Ausangate 33, 59–60
Aymara people 17, 39
Aztec people 16

Bacata 27
balance of nature 51, 52, 59, 60
balsa 39
bamboo 21
bananas 21, 32
barley 21
beech forests 57
Bellavista National Park 36, 55
Benalcázar, Sebastián de 32
biosphere reserve 34
birds 28, 34, 47, 48, 56

Bogotá, Colombia 8, 24, 27, 59
bola 48
Bolívar, Simón 24, 36
Bolivia 4, 8, 9, 12, 15, 17, 19, 20, 33, 35–41, 42, 43, 51, 53, 55
Bolivian Chaco 36
Boyacá, Colombia 24
Brasilia, Brazil 8
Brazil 8, 14, 25, 26, 27, 33, 36, 46, 48, 59
bromeliads 21
Buenos Aires, Argentina 8, 46

cacao 21, 32
Calí, Colombia 27, 51
California condor 53–54
Callao, Peru 33, 58
Cape Horn 4, 8
Caracas, Venezuela 8, 26
Caribbean Sea 6, 8, 12, 15, 25, 26, 27, 28
Catholicism 39
cattle 22, 23, 48, 51, 54
Cauca River 27, 28
Cayenne, French Guiana 8
Central America 16, 27
Central Railway 12
Central Valley 42, 44
Chile 4, 6, 7, 8, 9, 12, 15, 17, 19, 20, 33, 35, 37, 42–45, 46, 50, 53, 54, 55, 56
Chimborazo 29, 31
Chimbote, Peru 33–34
chocolate 32
climate 22, 32, 46, 47–48
clothing 18, 60
cloud forest 21, 31
coast 20, 25
coastal ranges 43
coca 28, 51
cocaine 28, 51
coffee 28
Colombia 4, 8, 15, 17, 24, 25, 26, 27, 29, 33, 51, 54, 59
colonization 23, 25
Columbus, Christopher (Cristóbal Colón) 8, 17, 23, 26, 27, 31
Concepción, Chile 8
condors 53–54
conservation 54, 55, 56
cooperatives 23
copper 19, 35, 39
cordillera 4
Cordillera Central 8, 27, 28–29, 33
Cordillera de la Costa 26, 55–56
Cordillera de Mérida 8, 26
Cordillera Occidental 8, 27, 33, 36, 37
Cordillera of the Andes (Cordillera de los

Andes) 4, 8, 42, 46, 50, 60
Cordillera Oriental 8, 27–28, 33, 36, 37
Cordillera Real 8, 33, 36, 37, 40
corn 21, 22
Costa 29, 31, 33, 52–53
Cotopaxi 8, 29, 31, 55
cougar 56
Cuenca, Ecuador 29
current 11
Cuzco, Peru 11, 17, 33, 35
cypress trees *see* alerce

dam 57
Darwin, Charles 4, 29, 31
deer 53, 54
Defoe, Daniel 57
Desaguadero River 36, 39
desert 9, 35, 43
domestic animals 55, 57
drainage basins 37
drought 17, 23
drugs, illegal 51
dung 51, 60
Dutch 26

Earth Summit 59
earthquakes 6, 34, 43, 44
ecology 51, 52, 53, 54, 55, 57
ecosystem 34, 59
Ecuador 4, 6, 8, 14, 15, 18, 24, 25, 27, 29–32, 33, 52, 55
El Niño 11–12
El Tatio Geyser Field 12
English 26
environment 50, 51, 59
epiphytes 21
equator 28, 29, 32, 35, 48
Equatorial Counter Current 9, 11
erosion 7, 51–52, 59
Esquel, Argentina 15, 46
Europe 14, 18, 23, 24, 51
Europeans 16, 18, 20, 23, 27, 44, 48
Everest, Mount 6
evergreens 21
evolution 29, 31
extinction 53

famine 17
farming 20, 21–23, 44, 51, 57, 59
farmland 22–23
fishing 11, 34
fog 21
forest industry 45
forests 21, 23, 25, 36, 44–45, 51–52, 54, 57
France 24, 44
French Guiana 8
fuel 60

Galápagos Islands 29, 31, 55
Galápagos Islands National Park 55
gauchos 48
geology 6, 29, 31
Georgetown, Guyana 8
Germans 44
glaciers 7, 9, 12, 36, 57
gold 19, 32, 35, 46
Gran Chaco 36, 46
Gran Colombia 24
grasslands 9, 28, 51
grazing 23, 51
Great Britain 32
guanaco 50
Guayaquil, Ecuador 29
Guayas River 29, 32
guira cuckoos 47
Gulf of Guayaquil 29, 32
Gulf of Panama 8
Gulf of San Jorge 8
Gulf of San Matias 8
Gulf of Venezuela 26
Guyana 8, 25

habitat 53, 54
haciendas 22, 23
Henri Pittier National Park 26, 55–56
herders 51
herons 28
highlands 12, 25, 31
Himalayas 6
horses 48
Houston, Charles S. 6
Huascarán, Mount 8, 33–34
huemul deer 54
Huila, Mount 27, 28
Humboldt (Peru) Current 9, 11
hummingbirds 22
hunting 34, 53 59

Iberians 18
Ice Age 37
Iguazú (Iguaçu) Falls 46, 48, 49
Illimani 8, 36, 40
immigrants 18, 32, 40, 44
Incas 12, 16–17, 19, 29, 32, 35, 39, 40, 56
independence 24
Ingapirca ruins 29
Iquitos, Peru 8, 12, 33
iron 35
irrigation 23
Isiboro-Securé National Park 36, 55
Isla de Chloé, Chile 42
Isla de San Andres, Colombia 27
Isla del Sol, Bolivia 39
Isthmus of Panama 8, 12, 16, 27

63

Juan Fernandez National Park 56, 57
jungles 25

La Condamine, Charles-Marie de 29
La Paz, Bolivia 8, 32, 35–36, 37, 40, 55
lakes 9, 12, 37, 39
languages 17, 20
Lauca National Park 42, 55, 56
lava 6, 28
lead 35, 40
lesser rhea 48
lichens 21
life zones 21
Lima, Peru 8, 12, 33, 58–59
livestock 20, 22, 39, 48
llama 9, 22, 37, 50, 56, 60
Llanos 8, 26, 27, 28
Los Alerces National Park 46, 57, 60
Los Glacieres National Park 46, 57
lowlands 25
lungs 40

Machángara River 32
Machu Picchu 11, 16, 33
Madre de Dios River 34
Magdalena River 27, 28
Magellan, Ferdinand 4
magma 7
Manú National Park 33, 34
Manú River 34
Mapocho River 44
Mapuche people 20
Maracaibo, Lake 8, 26
marine iguana 55
Maya 16
McIntyre, Loren 18–19, 31
Medellín, Colombia 27, 51
medicine 51
Mérida, Venezuela 26
mestizos 18, 19, 32, 40
Mexico 16, 42
minerals 19, 32, 35, 40
mining 19–20, 39–40, 51, 59
Misti, Mount 33, 34
Moche civilization 12
Mochima National Park 25, 26
Molina, Slaye 27
monastery 25
montaña 33
montane rain forest *see* cloud forest
Monterey pine 45
Montevideo, Uruguay 8
Morris, Arthur 44
moss 21
mountain climbing 6, 18, 47
mountain lions 34, 56
mountains 15, 17, 18, 25, 26, 28, 31

Nahuel Huapí National Park 46, 57

national parks 34, 55–57
natural resources 60
naturalists 54, 55–56
New Granada 24
"New World" 23, 26
Niagara Falls 48, 49
Nicaragua 27
Nile River 14
North America 6, 14, 16, 42, 46, 48, 51

oil 26, 27, 32, 34, 52–53
oil pipelines 52–53
Ojos del Salado, Mount 8, 42, 43
orchids 21, 34
Oriente 29, 31, 36
Orinoco River 26
Osorno, Volcano 7, 42
Otavalo, Ecuador 18
overcrowding 18, 27, 39, 58
oxygen 11, 40

Pachacuti, emperor 16
Pacific Ocean 4, 7, 8, 9, 27, 29, 31, 33, 34, 36, 42, 43, 46
pack animals 56, 60
palm trees 21
Pampas (Pampa) 8, 14, 46, 48
Panama 27
Panama Canal 17
Panama hat 32
panther 56
Paraguay 8, 36, 46
Paramaribo, Suriname 8
páramos life zone 22
Paraná River 48
pardo 27
parrots 34
pasture 54
Patagonia 8, 15, 45, 46, 47, 54, 56, 57
Patagonian Desert 14-15
Peru 4, 8, 9, 11, 12, 15, 16, 17, 20, 22, 23, 24, 27, 29, 31, 33–35, 36 39, 42, 51, 59
Peru Current *see* Humboldt Current
petroleum 26
Pico Bolívar 8, 26
pino distinguido 45
Pizarro, Francisco 32, 35
plains 25, 36
plants 11, 21, 29, 48, 55
plateau 9, 27, 34
plates, tectonic 7
poaching 55, 56
pollution 51, 58, 60
Poopó, Lake 36, 39
Portugal 23
Portuguese 17, 18
potatoes 21, 22
Potosí, Bolivia 37
pottery 16
Pucón, Chile 43
pudu 53
puma 55, 56

Puna 34
Punta Arenas, Chile 4, 42

Quechua 17, 19, 20, 40, 46
Quijos River 29, 31
Quito, Ecuador 8, 18, 19, 29, 31, 32

radiata pine 45
railroads 11, 19, 36, 58
rain forest 52
ranchers 54
red ibis 28
"red tide" 11
reforestation 45, 51
revolutions 23–24
Ring of Fire 7
Río de la Plata 8, 46, 48
ritual sacrifice 17
river systems 28, 31–32
rivers 20, 26, 35, 39, 45
roads 19, 36, 58
Robinson Crusoe 56–57
rocks 14
Rocky Mountains 6
"Royal Range" 33, 37
Ruiz, Mount 27, 28
rural areas 18, 40, 58

Sajama, Mount 8, 36, 37
San Martín, José de 24
San Rafael Falls 31
sand 25, 43
Sangay 6, 7, 29, 31, 55
Santiago, Chile 6, 8, 42, 44
semidesert 43–44
sheep 22, 23, 37, 56, 57
ships 4
shrimp 32
Siberia 16
Sierra 8, 29, 31
Sierra de Perijá 8, 26
silver 19, 35, 37, 43, 46
slash-and-burn agriculture 44–45
slaves 23
soil 14, 22, 44, 45, 51–52
Solís, Juan Díaz de 48
South America 4, 9, 11, 12, 14, 16, 17, 18, 19, 20, 22, 23, 26, 29, 32, 33, 35, 46, 47, 50, 51, 53, 56, 58
South American condor *see* Andean condor
South Pole 46
Spain 23, 24, 35, 48
Spanish 17, 18, 20, 25, 29 35, 37, 40, 44, 48
spectacled bear 34
spoonbills 28
Strait of Magellan 4, 8, 42, 46
Sucre, Bolivia 8, 36
sugarcane 21
Sun Temple 17
Supreme Court of Bolivia 36
Suriname 8
swamps 36

tapir 60
temperate zone 47
temperature 11, 44
Tierra del Fuego 4, 8, 42, 46
Tihuanaco, Bolivia 17
tin 19, 39
Titicaca, Lake 8, 9, 15, 22, 33, 36, 37–39, 40
tobacco 21
Torres del Paine National Park 12, 42 ,56
tortoise, giant 31
tortora reeds 39
tourism 31, 43, 55, 56
Trancura River 45
tree ferns 21
tropical forests 21, 36
tuna 11

U.N. Food and Agriculture Organization 51
underground springs 43
UNESCO 34
United Nations 59
United Nations' World Heritage List 57
United States 6, 26
urban areas 27, 39, 40 58–59
Urubamba Canyon 11
Urubamba River 12
Uruguay 8, 46
Uruguay River 48
Ushuaia 46

Valley of the Moon 9
valleys 15, 32, 43
Valparaíso, Chile 42
vegetables 22
Venezuela 5–6, 8, 15, 23, 24, 25–27, 51, 55–56
Vespucci, Amerigo 26
vicuña 55, 56
Villa de San Francisco de Quito 32
Villarica volcano 42, 43
Viracocha 17
volcanic eruptions 6, 34
volcanoes 6, 7, 12, 15, 28, 31, 32, 34, 37, 43, 47

waterfall 48
watersheds 37
weather 35
Western Hemisphere 6
wetlands 28
wheat 21
white people 27, 32
wildlife 12, 21, 31, 34, 53–54, 55
wind 46, 47
wool 37

Yungay, Peru 34

zinc 35, 40
Zurbriggen, Matthias 47